Stud of the Huds

A Swim in Twenty Stages

Thank you
Tim
Johnson

By
Captain Tim Johnson, PE
Assistant Professor
Department of Electronics and Mechanical
Wentworth Institute of Technology
550 Huntington Ave.
Boston, Massachusetts, 02115

First Printing: March, 2006 by Lightning Source, Inc.

Other Books by the Author

Finding a Job in Tough Times, 2002
History of Open-Water Marathon Swimming, 2004

Cover photo by Fred Sahlberg, Public Safety Director of Bergen Community College, of Skip Storch in the upper reaches of the Hudson River.

The author extends his thanks to Andrew Clarke, John Parriott, Bob Peters, and Adam Palmer for their assistance during the writing of this play.

Publisher:
Captain's Engineering Services
Buzzards Bay, MA 02532
(www.captainsengsvc.com)

COPYRIGHT © 2006 Captain's Engineering Services
All rights reserved. No part of this book may be reproduced, in any form or by any means, without the permission in writing from the publisher. While the information present herein is factually true as it relates to the swim recounted; names, persons, conversations, actions, activities recounted may not wholly or in part represent actual occurrences.

ISBN 0-9721726-3-7

Play Synopsis

When marathon swimmer Skip Storch learns the Hudson River swim record is held by a dog; he takes $10,000 out of the bank, books a boat, and starts stroking! Along the way he confronts confounding tides, adverse weather, alcoholic support crews, invasive fauna, mechanical failures, financial woes, physical exhaustion to see a successful swim strategy emerge. From Albany, NY, to the Battery at the foot of Manhattan, Skip keeps up a relentless swim schedule of two-hour swims twice a day, one in the morning and one in the evening. After falling behind at the start, he pulls even with the dog's pace at the Tappan Zee Bridge nine days into the schedule. The final two swims deliver up the missing ingredient, current, strong and fast. Skip finishes the swim with two amazing stages that clinches the record, beating the dog.

Cast of Characters:

SD: Tim Johnson, the Swim Director.
SS: Skip Storch, the swimmer.
Sally: Sally Masterson, Licensed Massage Therapist.
Don: Don Shultz, Commodore of the Albany Yacht Club:
Captain Fred Sahlberg, owner of RoJo, a 30' cabin cruiser.
Kara: Kara Kozen, Athletic Trainer Certified.
Ed S: Ed Skillman, Dock master at Albany Yacht Club.
Dockboy: Catskill marina attendant
Doug: Doug Sheppard, NY State DEC employee
Waitress and Chief in Catskill.
Dolly, Sally's girlfriend.
CP: Captain Brian Pickering, owner of Magic Moment
Ed: Ed Prigge 3rd, 1st Mate on Magic Moment.
Rosemary, owner of a bed and breakfast
Red: Red Grenier, owner of Sunset, a support boat.
Jim: Jim Irving, owner of Runabout II, a support boat.
Andy: Andrea Waronker, Skip's wife.
Tank: Tank Sherman, a boat owner at Haverstraw marina.
Bryan: Bryan Juncosa, owner of NoName, a support boat.
Roger: Roger Muller, a college friend of Skip.

Table of Contents

Prelude

Scene 1 An idea is born

Scene: in a side corner of a living room, the SD is before a portable computer at a secretariat. It's late at night during the fall of 2004. The SD is accessing data base information from the NY Times.

SD (calls out): Okay, Darling, you go to bed; I'm going to stay up and work on my swim book.

(Turns to computer)

SD: Here's one I can use: *50-Hour Record is Set in Swim from Albany.* Looks good.

SD: Here's another: *Swimmer Hooper at Hudson.* Wonder who Hooper is?

SD: What's this? *A Dog Swims from Albany in Record Time*. This is a curiosity; can't be true. I've got to read this.

SD reads out loud the article and then stops and ponders.

"Lucky, a three year old German Shepard dog, completed her 153 mile swim from Albany to Manhattan shortly after 11 am yesterday morning…(SD pondering: The dog's name is Lucky?) Her swimming time for the whole route was forty four hours forty five minutes…about five hours faster than the human record held by George Creegan…John Schweighart, a baker from the Bronx, said he was proud of his dog…with Vincent Astor's new yacht (SD pondering: Astor's yacht? It must have been on hell of a strudel this baker could make)…Lucky dived yelping into the water on the last lap of her journey. Once in the water she was silent, swimming swiftly and breathing through her mouth like a human…if she stayed in the water more than an hour she would swim on her side for relaxation."

SD (pondering): The dog could swim sidestroke? How can a dog swim faster than a human? Why would anyone make a dog swim that far?

SD: A dog can not swim faster than a human! If this is true, how did they do it?

SD draws a current flow on a chalkboard (sine wave), draws a line horizontally thru the middle of it, and labels the top portion the flood and the bottom the ebb.

SD: Let's see, staged swims: the swimmer starts swimming at slack water then swims until the next slack water. Each swim is about six hours long. The swimmers average push is 70% of the

Markimum rated current flow for that day. They are done in about 5 days if they swim on both tides.
SD (pondering): Why did the dog take so many days? He must have been swimming shorter portions of the flow.
SD back at the board.
SD: Suppose I put a swimmer in here (makes vertical slashes delineating the peak of the sine wave). God, this is brilliant. He gets the best water. Why swim when the water is dead?
SD starts writing his thoughts on the computer, lights dim.

Scene 2 A plan is developed
SD is on the phone with Skip in late winter of 2005.
SD: Skip, I've published a book on swimming.
SS: No kidding?
SD: Yes, it's called *History of Open-Water Marathon Swimming.*
SS: Am I in the book?
SD: You're a big part of it.
SS: Cuba?
SD: The whole story.
SS: Maroney?
SD: Exposed.
SS: She ruined that swim. Everybody believes she did it.
SD: She's in the chapter on Bogus Swims.
SS: That's great. I was out of shape on my swim and had an upset stomach from some food I ate there.
SD: Skip, I've always said that if the swimmer is the organizer, the swim suffers. Just to get into Cuba took you two years.
SS: I know.
SD: You're the best organizer I know. You think of everything.
SD: (quietly) I had to include some of your swims in there.
SS: What do you mean?
SD: Your environmental swims.
SS: You know, I had an impossible schedule to keep. What about my East River swim?
SD: That's the enigma. Swims like that are totally legitimate. Even Suzy's record double across the Channel is included.
SS: My Hudson River swim was creditable. I did it in 53 hours.
SD: I wasn't able to verify it; I wasn't on the swim.
SS: Tim, I have a video of it. Jane was on it.
SD: I'm not doubting it.

SS: All right.
SD: Skip, while I was researching my book I discovered something unusual about the Hudson River swims.
SS: There were only 11 people that have swum it. The record was by George Creegan of 50 hours set in 1927. What did you find?
SD: A dog swam the Hudson.
SS: Go on, you're kidding me.
SD: No really, I found a report in the NY Times, about a paragraph long that said a dog in 1928 swam the river in 44 hours.
SS: 44 hours? That's impossible.
SD: It might be but I think I've figured out how the dog did it.
SS: How do we know he did it?
SD: We don't. All we have is the report. It says that he took 22 days.
SS: You know, in my Long Island swim, a dog on the lobster boat swam out to me. Did you see that? That picture went around the world.
SD: I remember the dog in the Long Island Sound. The fishing boat had a nice rig to retrieve him.
SS: How'd they get the dog to swim a course?
SD: I'm not sure how he got the dog to swim the course, but the key to unlocking the speed is the fact that it took 22 days.
SS: Why so long?
SD: The dog only swam during the peak hours of the tide. I believe he swam two hours a day.
SS: So he wouldn't swim as far as I did when I swam from slack water to slack water.
SD: Yes, but he's averaging a faster current than you. You would only get 70% of the current flow on average while the dog would get nearly 95%.
SS: That's brilliant, suppose I swim 3 hours.
SD: It drops the average push from the current. You only need two hours.
SS: My regular workout is 2 hours.
SD: You'd have to swim twice a day, on every outgoing tide.
SS: Why twice a day?

SD: The monthly tide cycle has two fast weeks and two slow weeks. If you go during the two fast weeks, you have to finish before the current slows down.
SS: Send me a schedule of what you think I could do. I'm going to give this some serious thought.
SD: Gotcha. Can you imagine a dog swimming faster than a human?
SS: Hey, I've got a dog that can swim faster than you!
Skip and Tim hang up laughing.

Stage 1

Scene 1 The start

Location: Albany Yacht Club, found 1873. Late afternoon on a sunny day in Albany along the Hudson River waterfront a small crowd including television crew and personality gathers on the docks of the Albany Yacht Club. Three casual visitors from a mega yacht stopped by and SD is talking in hushed tones in the background, Don Schultz and his wife along with the dock master. Fred Sahlberg the owner and captain of RoJo, Sally, and Kara stand about. Skip steps to the microphone of Channel 12 Regional News and the cameras are rolling:

SS (speaking to the camera): This swim represents a journey. When I first swam the Hudson River in 1988 it was in the name of the environment…

SD (to the observers): The human record is fifty hours; Skip did it in fifty-three.

SS (speaking to the camera): I want to thank my wife, Andrea, …

SD (to the observers): A dog swam the river in 1928 and did it in 44 hours.

The observers do a double take and then listen closely to Skip.

SS (speaking to the camera): There are people I want to mention, Sally Masterson.

Sally (stepping up to the camera): I'm a massage therapist and I …

SD (to Don): Thanks for helping me get a new cell phone today.

Don: It was nothing, Tim.

SD: Don, it took two hours of your life, I've had babies delivered faster. Since you're the Vice-Commandant of the yacht club I thought I'd mention that every swim down the Hudson started at this yacht club.

Don: When was the first swim?

SD: 1888 by Steve Brodie.

Don: The club was on the other side of the river back then. We're now in Rensselaer

SD (glancing across the river): Really? That sort of changes the start; well, it's a small detail since you're only across the river from the original start. What I wanted to say is that there's been a close association between swimmers and the club for over a century.

SS (speaking to the camera): This swim represents a second chance for me. To comprehend the drive that pushes me to attempt this is to know the artistic medium I work in: marathon swimming. I use my heart, muscles, mind, and my passion. It's a different kind of expression but it's true to me and defines me as a free person in America. In this swim, my team and I will be focused on the goal. Together we will…
Fred: Tim, here are some lifejackets. These are the type that inflates if they are immersed in water.
SD (putting it on): Oh, nice ones. Thanks.
Fred: Don, can you take the press out for photos of the swim?
Don: Sure.
SS (speaking to the camera): It's time to make a comeback, from a broken body, a paralyzed arm, and a disease called sarcoidosis. I feel great. I've trained for this my whole life…
SD: Skip, three minutes.
SS (speaking to the camera): It's time to break the record. Kara, tide waits for no man, woman, or beast.
SD: Kara, you get in the dinghy first and get comfortable. Sit in the front. Oh, put the lifejacket on, the Albany police launch is coming along as our escort and we want to look legal.
Skip puts on his goggles and nose clip; SD starts the count down from the dinghy. The photographers wait to photograph the start then board Don's boat, which had been pressed into service.
Kara: 5, 4, 3, 2, 1, Go.
Flashbulb pop…dinghy moves off

Scene 2 Aboard the dinghy
The dinghy is seen on the river with SD and Kara aboard. Background video or photos of shoreline of the Hudson out of Albany. Dilapidated dock, cement plants, working boats, noisy, and in the background is the steady plop-plop of Skips stoking. Swimmer is not seen, only heard while swimming.
SD: Do you have the stopwatch?
Kara: Yes
SD: Do you have the schedule of when he wants the whistle and horn blown?
Kara: Yes
SD: I'm going to try and push him more toward the center.

Fred (on VHF): Swimmer escort, swimmer escort, the northbound tug requests you stay on the eastern side of the river.
SD (on VHF): Affirmative.
SD gestures to attract Skip's attention. Skip stops swimming
SD: Skip, we have to swim closer to the shore.
SS: I can't hear you.
Kara: We have to move, there's a tug coming.
SS: Okay.
Skip resumes swimming.
SD: Where is this tug, do you see it?
Kara: No
Kara blows the whistle, SD looks at the GPS.
SD: Kara, what is your role with this swim?
Kara: I'm the athletic trainer. I stretch Skip before and after he swims.
SD: How old are you?
Kara: I'm twenty-four.
Kara blows the signal horn. Tim reads the distance on the GPS.
SD: I can't get the VHF radio to squelch.
Tim maneuvers the dinghy over by the police launch.
SD (to the police launch): Can you guys get this VHF to operate correctly; the squelch is going to drain the battery.
SD hands the VHF to the police launch as they go by. Tim maneuvers the dinghy back to the swimmer.
Kara blows another whistle.
SD: Skip's doesn't seem to be going very fast. I'm reading one point nine knots.
Police launch comes alongside and hands the VHF back to Tim.
SD: Testing, 1, 2, 3.
No response, Tim waves down Fred and tries again.
SD (on VHF): Testing 1, 2, 3.
SD (to Kara): They didn't fix the squelch; they just turned the volume down.
Fred (maneuvers his boat nearby): How's Skip doing?
SD: Something is wrong. The current doesn't seem to be up. We should be doing two point seven knots. Right now we're below two knots.
Fred: What do you suggest?
SD: Wait for the second half hour and compare the distances. If it's not building then we've missed the current.

SS (stops swimming): Which way?
SD gestures and shouts a tug is coming.
SS resumes swimming.
SD: This tug is taking one heck of a long time.
Kara blows another whistle and stares intently at Skip.
Kara: Any goldfish crackers around?
SD: Check the blue bag. Could you hand me a bottle of water?
Kara: Tim, there's a log up ahead.
SD: Kara, just take the net and push it out of the way. I'll try and move him off to the right with the dinghy.
Kara sticks the net into the water and prods a log out of Skip's path.
(Later)
SD (sounding perturbed): There's the tug. Looks like he's pulling into shore to tie up. We've been pushed out of the channel all this time for no reason.
A bit later, Kara blows the signal horn at the end of the 1st hour.
SD: We're stopping the swim here, there's no point in swimming in this slow water.
Kara (waving her arms): Skip, Skip, hold up.
SD signals with suggestive hand signaling for Fred to pick up the swimmer.
As RoJo pulls up, Skip asks…
SS: Are the props stopped?
Fred: Yes.
Fred: Skip, use the swim ladder.
Tim and Kara drop the marker, grappling hook, line and marker. Then return to the stern of RoJo.
SS (from stern of RoJo): What happened?
SD: I think the current turned on you and is flowing north. You only made two miles in one hour.
SS (patiently): This was the shakedown swim.
SD (frustrated): I'm having a technological nightmare here. I can't get the VHF to work right, the GPS doesn't have a waypoint, my new cell phone is impossible, and my tide program is out of whack; I'm going to have to break down and read the manuals.

Scene 3 Recovery

The RoJo is tied up at Albany Yacht Club. Tim is seen reading the manuals for the VHF and the GPS and testing them. The girls are sitting about chatting to each other. Tim gets up and goes inside the salon of RoJo where Skip is resting by lying down on the sofa, cushions abound.

SS (lying on the sofa, speaking to Tim): When do we begin the next stage?

SD (pushing some gear aside to sit in the chair opposite the sofa, he's looking at his portable computer): Ebb was supposed to begin at 1 pm so the 4:30 start today was just before peak. We didn't get a good current. I suspect that the flood started during your swim because here at the dock when we returned, the current was all ready flowing north. It isn't supposed to start until 9:30 pm tonight. I think the tide is 3.5 hours off from the predictions.

SS: What are we going to do if we can't trust the predictions?

SD: I'm going to have to watch for the current to switch. That will pin the time we start to two hours later.

SS: Tim, you didn't answer me, what time should we start?

SD: Skip, right now, if the tide switched to flood at 5pm, and the flood up in Albany lasts for only 5 hours, ebb will be at 10pm or so, figure on a 12 pm start with 11pm wake-up. We'll wake you up. Better get to bed.

SS (calling out to Fred in the kitchen): Fred, what are the sleeping arrangements?

Fred: The girls have the V-berth and Skip is on the couch in the main salon.

SS (aside to the guys): You know Sally is a lesbian.

SD: This is awkward.

Fred (excited): Then she can sleep with the guys.

Later, Fred and Tim are seen standing on the stern of RoJo.

Fred: Tim, this doesn't leave many places for us to sleep. The two captains are without a bunk.

SD: Fred, this afternoon's swim was so screwed up I'm going to have to stay up all night just to watch the tide switch. I can't let something like that happen again, it'll kill the swim.

Fred: Tim, I don't know that much about swimming, how has this affected the swim?

SD: In all the history of swimming the Hudson, this was the worst start ever recorded.
Fred: So Skip had a bad start.
SD: You could say that. Right now, he's given everybody a head start.
Fred: What do you mean?
SD: Everyone who has swum this river went farther in the first leg than Skip and we're trying an unproven strategy to set a record.
Fred: Sounds like the pressure is on.
SD: This start has certainly put the outcome in doubt. Oh, there's Don, I've got to ask him some questions.
Don: Hello, Tim.
SD: Don, would you know any reason the tide would be off?
Don: Well, the locks are open.
SD: The locks are open?
Don: Yes, when there is a lot of rain, they open the locks at Troy to lower the water level upstream.
SD: Holy mackerel that would explain things.
Don: What?
SD: The current is not flowing on schedule according to the tide programs.
Don: Oh, sure with all the water dumping out it always changes the water flow.
SD: Thanks, Don.
SD rejoins Fred on the stern of RoJo.
SD (looking down river): You know, it's hard to believe this small river here turns into the Hudson River I'm use to around Manhattan.
Fred: The Hudson doesn't look like much here. What did you find out?
SD: Don says the locks are open.
Fred (shocked surprise): That could have an effect on the swim. What are you going to do?
SD: I've got to wait and watch the current. We're at the mercy of the river.
Later, Fred and Tim are on the stern of RoJo.
Fred: It's 10 o'clock.
SD: Let me take a look at the current.

SD (shining a light on the water flowing by the dock): The current is roaring north, just look at that flotsam!
Fred and Tim (later, dark):
Fred: Its 11 o'clock, are we going to wake up Skip?
SD (glancing at the water): No, not with the current running the way it is.
Fred: Why don't you try and get some rest?
Tim: Okay, I'll try and get comfortable in this deck chair. Wake me at midnight.
Tim tries to get comfortable in a folding chair.
(Later still)
Tim: Fred, how's the current running.
Fred (glancing out at the river): North
Tim: I might as well get up; I'm not getting any sleep.
Tim (looking at the river): This is really slow but it's still going north. I'm going to wander around and try to find some current markers.
Fred: What are those?
SD: Oh, pieces of wood or something I can watch float by and time it over a known distance.
Tim goes off to look for wood. Fred sits by the river in the moonlight on a spectacular evening.
(Later, about 1 pm)
SD: Fred, I've never seen anything like this. It's 1 am and the current is still flowing north, slowly but its flowing north. This makes it eight hours that the current has been flooding.
Fred: (mutters something indistinguishable)
SD: I couldn't find that piece of wood I put aside earlier but I found some pretzel sticks.
Fred: Pretzels, do you think they will work?
SD: If they float, they should work. In the English Channel, I used an orange. In a 39 knots wind with 16-foot waves, I got my current simulator to match up perfectly with the data we collected.
Fred: When were you over at the Channel?
SD: About 3 years ago. I was testing some theories.
Fred: That's pretty horrific conditions.
SD: That's not the half of it! I was in a 30-foot sailboat with Roger Barlick, the owner. We had one reef in when we left Dover. When it was time to go back, we decide to put a 2nd reef

in. He went forward, had a little bit of trouble dropping the sail so he stepped back to the rail to look up the mast. Just as he looked up, the boat heeled and he did a perfect back dive off the boat.

Fred: Oh, my god!

SD: Well, we were doing everything right: we were headed up into the wind, idling to just hold a position so when I looked over the side, there he was but two strokes from the stern. I threw him a line and he stepped aboard sans his glasses and wallet.

Fred: He was lucky.

SD: As it was happening, it was like slow motion and I was thinking, "...he's going over...nice dive...I'm not bring this boat back in by myself...What the hell will I tell his wife?"

Fred and Tim (about 2 pm)

SD: Fred, it's switched.

SD (looking at his watch): At 2:20 am the current switched to ebb. The swim is at 4:30 am. This river has corrected itself in one tide. What an extraordinary event. Too bad it screwed the swim up.

Fred: Let's see if we can get some shuteye, I'm going up on the bridge. Are you going to get some sleep?

SD: Probably not.

Fred: Call me at 4 am; it won't take us that long to get there.

SD: No problem.

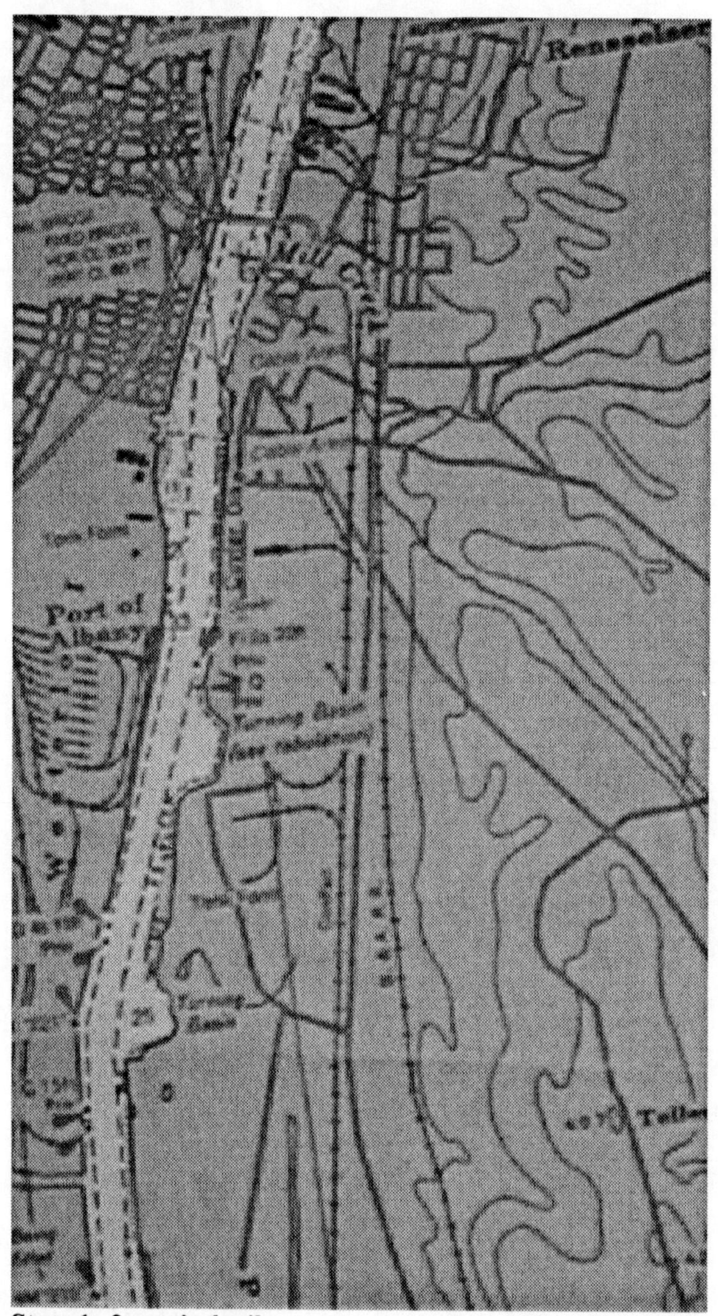

Stage 1 2 nautical miles.

Stage 2

Scene 1 Disaster strikes

Tuesday, August 16th, AM swim with a schedule 4 am start. Weather is clear and calm. Sun comes up at the end. Scene opens with crew in the dinghy in the dark. Tim and Kara are puttering about in the darkness looking for the marker with a torch (flashlight) just before 4 am.

Tim: See the marker?

Kara: There it is.

Tim: River is running good. Missed it. I'll come around again.

Kara: Tim, you still have about 5 feet to go.

Tim: Something's wrong. I can't get the boat to move.

Tim (on VHF): RoJo, I don't' have any control over the dinghy.

Fred (on VHF): We'll come along side and I'll check it out.

Fred boards the dinghy after Tim and Kara get out.

Fred: The propeller has spun-off, no wonder you aren't going anywhere.

Sally: What will we do about the swim?

SS: I can swim off the mother ship.

Fred: Let me get the marker aboard and then we'll start the swim.

SS: Sounds good.

Fred makes two passes before they give up. SD is playing with the GPS.

SD: Fred, let's get Skip swimming and forget about the marker, the current is moving very strong right now.

Fred: Okay

SD: I've figured out how the GPS can waypoint the finishing location. I've marked this spot all ready.

(Later)

Skip is swimming off of RoJo. Sally and Kara are sitting on the bow. Fred and Tim are in the flying bridge.

SD: We've got a little fog this morning.

Fred: One of the hazards of navigation.

SD: It shouldn't make that much difference to the swimmer.

Sally (calls up to the bridge): Skips is working too hard. He's lifting his head to check the course.

SD (calls down to the bow): When we're not right there next to him, he going to do that.

Skip (stops swimming): Which way?

SD and Sally gesture, both point ahead. Skip resumes swimming.
Sally reads the stopwatch and blows a signal horn.
SD: Fred, do we have any river traffic?
Fred: I made the security announcement and haven't heard anything yet.
SS (stops swimming): Which way?
Sally and Tim both stand up and point forward. Skip resumes swimming.

Scene 2 Salon scene after the swim
(Later, after the swim, up on the flying bridge of RoJo)
SD: Skip made a little over four miles in this swim so the current doesn't seem to be very strong.
Fred: After we tie up in Albany, I'm going to catch some shut-eye in the vee-berth.
Tim: I think I'll join you.
(After tying up in Albany, in the salon of RoJo)
Sally and Kara proceed to work on Skip giving him a rubdown on the couch. Sally climbs all over Skip and the couch to get into the right positions. Kara, the physical therapist holds court on the floor and works him over too. Tim goes by climbing over items on his way to the forward vee berth. Fred follows along behind.
Fred: Skip, what's the reason for the rubdown.
SS: They are deep massaging my muscles to get the lactic acid out of the tissue.
SD (muttering): You lucky stiff.
SD (to Fred): It sure is crowded in here.
Fred: Skip put all his gear on board and it's taking up half the salon.
SD: That's going to make things rather tight. Where's the wastebasket?
Skip: There's one down in the galley.
SD (in the galley): There's not a spot unoccupied here. I've never seen such clutter
Fred: Just as long as I can get my coffee in the morning.
SD and Fred retire to bed in the vee-berth.
Skip and Sally are talking together as she works him over.

SS: Sally, we have to work out a system because I can't hear Tim.
Sally: I'll say.
SS: This stopping to ask questions slows me down. If you hold your hand up, palm toward the bow, it means swim away from the boat. Holding your hand up toward the stern means swim to the boat.
Sally: Okay, we'll try it this afternoon.
Kara (to SS): I've got to go to work this afternoon.
SS: Give Tim your cell number so he can advise you of where we will be at so you can meet us.
Kara: Okay.

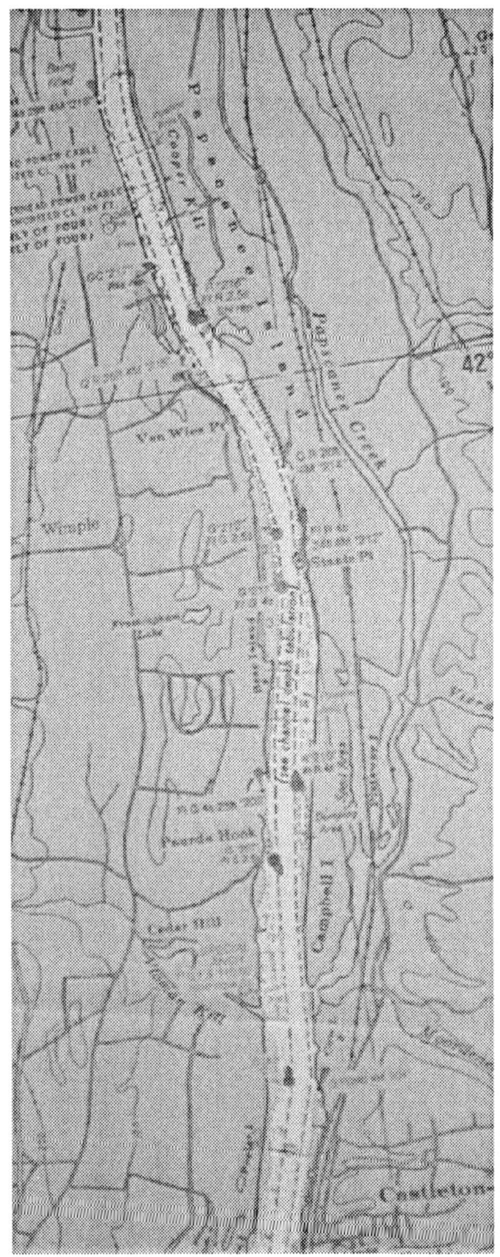

Stage 2 4.3 nautical miles.

Stage 3

Scene 1 Tuesday morning in Albany

Tuesday, August 16th, PM swim with a scheduled 4:30 pm start. Location: Albany Yacht Club dock about 10 am. A small 5 hp Mercury motor is lying on the dock minus its propeller. Sally joins Tim dockside. He is bent over the motor examining it.

Tim: Sally, I've got to get the motor fixed. The cotter pin holding the nut must have sheared off. I was going in and out of gear so many times that I must have stressed the mechanisms.

Sally: Let me see what I can do to help.

Sally goes off and finds the dock master of the Albany Yacht club, Ed Skillman, in his office.

Sally: We have a problem with our dinghy motor.

Ed S: What's the make?

Sally: I'm not sure; we have it sitting by the boat.

SD (joining the group): It's a Mercury 5 horsepower.

Ed S: Well, Mercury has a dealer about 10 miles from here, let me finish up a few items and I'll take you over there in my truck with the motor.

Tim (as they step out of the office): Sally, this is great, I'll go bring the motor up to his truck.

Fred (standing on RoJo, rubbing sleep from his eyes): Tim, what's happening?

SD (turning to Fred): Sally got the dock master interested in helping us out. He's taking the motor to a dealer.

Fred: I'm coming!

Tim: If you're going, I'm sacking out again.

Tim returns to the boat and bumps into Skip

SS: What time is the next start?

Tim: Wait a minute while I bring up the program to check. (Pause) It looks like a 5 pm start if the river has settled down.

SS: Great. Let's get some breakfast then some rest.

Kara: I've got my car here. I can take you.

SD: There's a diner around the corner from the yacht club. Fred and I went there for breakfast yesterday. The hash browns are the best.

SS: You know, if you could bring back some eggs and a hamburger, I'll stay here and rest.

SD: Okay, Skip. I'll bring some muffins back, too.

Scene 2 Sally's interview

Later, early afternoon on the dock alongside RoJo, Fred returns and calls out to Tim who is sitting on the stern of RoJo.

Fred: Tim, what time is Skip scheduled to start swimming?

SD: He's scheduled for a five pm start.

Fred: Let's head downriver closer to the start. We can get lunch at the marina that's located in the town of Castleton-on-the-Hudson. It's right nearby.

SD: Sounds good to me. Everything been accomplished here in Albany that we can.

With everyone aboard, Fred starts the engines and the lines are let go. The RoJo heads down river. Tim and Fred are talking on the bridge of the RoJo where Sally joins them later.

Fred: Tim, the Dock master really helped us out. That dealer was about 15 miles from here and a cab would have cost a fortune. Since the part is being delivered tomorrow, the Dock master will pick it up and bring it down to us at our next marina, Coeymans. So the RoJo will have to serve as the dinghy until tomorrow night.

SD: I'm telling you, the people in Albany must be known by their hospitality. We need to tip the dock master generously.

Fred: They've been very helpful. I'll make sure he's taken care of.

Sally (coming up the ladder): Any room topside?

SD: Sally, have a seat here, I'll move to the port side.

Sally: All right.

Fred: Nice to see you. How's Skip?

Sally: He's sleeping.

Fred: Sally, if you don't mind my asking; why are you a lesbian?

Sally (enjoying the opportunity): I wasn't happy when I was married. And it turned out that I enjoyed women more.

Fred: You certainly seen happy enough. Have you had any regrets?

Sally: Not since I met my girlfriend. I want to get married.

Fred: I want you to feel comfortable aboard the boat.

Sally: Thanks. You've been very welcoming.

Fred: You're a massage therapist.

Sally: Yes, I'm licensed here in New York.

Fred: What does this therapy do for Skip's swimming?

Sally: One, it relaxes and loosens him up. I can then increase his range of motion which allows him to breathe deeper and hold it. With the deep massaging, his circulation increases which will help remove the lactic acid. The main reason muscles tighten up after exertion is the lactic acid.
Fred: Wow, that's interesting.
(Later)
Fred: Tim, did you get any sleep?
SD: I hate to say this but based on the past 24 hours, sleep is overrated.
Sally (cocking her head and listening): What that noise?
Fred: It's some kind of vibration from the starboard engine. On the way up to Albany from Nyack, something happened to my starboard engine.
SD: Should we get it looked at?
Fred: If I keep the speed below 10 knots, the noise doesn't start up. I'll take care of it when I get back home.
SD: Okay.
(Later)
SD: This looks like the dock for Castleton.
Fred: I'll pull in right behind the gas pump. I'll need to leave room for another boat ahead of us.
SD: They have a crane for stepping masts. We'll have to leave room behind us in case a sailboat comes in.
Fred: What's that about?
SD: Further up the Hudson in the Erie Canal, there are low bridges that boats can't go under unless their masts are taken down.
Fred: So sailboats going to the Great Lakes need to have their masts stepped?
SD: Yes, and boats headed south have them put back in.
Fred: Looks like that's a thriving business along the river.
SD: It appears to be a service marinas try and provide along this stretch of the Hudson.
After tying up the boat at the dock,
SD: Everyone, the swim start is around four thirty pm.
SD (to Skip): Fred, Sally and I were going to walk uptown to get lunch. Want to come?
SS: No, I'll just stay here at the clubhouse and relax.
SD: Okay.

Scene 3 Rough water

Later after leaving Castleton, Fred and SD are on the flying bridge with RoJo underway.

SD (reading the GPS): Fred, we're coming up on the drop location. Just turn into the current and then we can drift a bit.

Skip appears on the swim platform then disappears into the water.

Sally (shouting so Skip can hear): 3, 2, 1, Go. Sally blows the signal horn.

Tim: Sara, I can spell you for a while with the whistle blowing. There's no need for you to sit out on the bow for the whole two hours. With the dinghy out of commission, I've not much to do.

Sally: Sounds great to me.

Sally blows the signal horn.

Sally (hollers up to me on the bridge from the bow): What's the distance?

SD: Let me check, I've got one point two miles.

Sally writes the distance down.

Fred: The bow babe is working!

SD: The bow babe? That's rich.

SD joins Sally on the bow.

SD: I'm seeing about a 2' chop mixed in with a 3'swell. This is pretty rough conditions for swimming. Wind is blowing just at 20 knots from the south.

Sally: I'll be putting him back together tonight.

SD: The wind is the main problem. If he keeps popping his head up to look ahead, his neck will give him problems again.

Sally: How can you tell the wind speed?

SD: When white caps begin to break out, it's blowing 18 knots. We have more than a few so it's a little faster.

Sally: Where'd you learn that?

SD: I sail as much as I use to swim.

(Later)

SD: He's getting away from the boat. We need to pull him in closer.

Sally holds her hand up toward the stern. Tim looks at this then notices Skip changes direction.

SD: What's going on?

Sally: When we hold our hand up toward the bow, it means for Skip to swim away from the boat. When we hold our hand up toward the stern, it means to come closer to the boat.
SD: Oh-h-h!
SD watches a train cross over the railroad bridge about 5pm as they approached the bridge.
(Later, during a lull in the swim)
Fred: There's a horrid smell coming from the kitchen.
Sally (calling up from the bow): It's not any of my stuff.
Fred: I think it's something Skip eats.
SD: And it smells?
Fred: Something awful.
(Later)
SD: From the looks of that weather front up ahead of us, I'm putting on my foul weather gear now.
Tim goes below to fetch his foul weather gear. Returns and puts the gear on pants and all.
Fred: You know it's not going to rain now.
Sally: Anyone got a raincoat.
Fred: I'll dig one out. Tim, take the helm for me.
SD: Okay.
A storm comes up and drenches the boat and its occupants with water. Fred gave Sally his wife's rain jacket and put his own on. We cruise by Coeymans, silently watching people on the veranda watching us. Evening descends on the river quietly.
Sally blows the signal horn twice.
SD: Let's get him out; the two hours are up.
Skip is extracted from the water and he goes into the salon for his rubdown.
Fred: How'd we do?
Tim (aside): Distance is not looking good, 4½ miles, something is wrong. I don't think Skip is swimming as fast as he told me he could.

Scene 4 Coeymans marina

Scene opens on the flying bridge of RoJo with Fred and SD.
Fred: Don Schultz up in Albany told me I have to enter from the south to avoid the rocks along the breaker. He says some boats try and go across the breaker and they wind up sinking.
SD: Humph, there are warning signs posted on the breaker.

Fred: Where should we tie up?
SD: Along this pier looks as good and I can see the electrical access boxes.
Fred: Great, that settles it, we can plug in. Tim, handle the lines?
SD: I'll go forward.
(Later in the salon of RoJo after tying up as Skip is being attended by Sally)
SS: I'll stay here on board; you all go ashore for a great meal. I need the rest.
SD: What would you like us to bring back?
SS: A hamburger would be great.
(SD sits down in the chair after moving excess gear aside.)
SD: Skip, when we discussed this swim you said you were swimming two miles an hour. Could we go over that again?
SS: Yes, I do the first mile in 25 minutes then drop down to about 28 minutes with the last mile in 35 minutes.
SD: Is that mile a swimmer's 66 laps of a 25-yard pool, a 1650?
SS: Yes.
SD: Okay, you're doing fine; I just need to revise my figures so that I can account for the current better. A 1650 is more like a statute mile, about 15% less than a nautical mile. You're doing something more like 1.7 knots.
SS: Should I swim faster?
SD: No, just pace it out, you've got a whole lot of river ahead of you. What's with the right hand placement in the water?
SS: After the hurricane in 98, I was a mess. My neck was broken, my arm was paralyzed, and then I developed sarcoidosis and wound up with my legs elevated for 3 months. This swim is really a comeback swim for me.
SD: You're looking good in the water. I'll keep an eye on the stroke and let you know if the right arm entry changes.
SS: With the rough water today, I had to kick more and now I'm resting with my legs up to ease any swelling from the sarcoidosis.
SD: Were you using the trudgeon?
SS: Actually, it was a double trudgeon. I would breathe on both sides for each stroke with the scissor kick. It's a specialty stroke for power and I need the extra oxygen for fuel.
SD: So you don't normally swim using that stroke?

SS: No, I'll use the American crawl and can breathe out of either side depending on where the pace boat is positioned.
Sally: Tim, let him get some rest now. Let's go eat.
SD: Okay, let me find Fred.
Tim goes back outside.
Fred (going thru one of Skip's supply cartons): Skip ate some disgusting smelly fish and it's stinking up the boat.
SD: I hadn't noticed.
Fred: Here it is!
Fred puts a can of sardines in a plastic garbage bag.
SD: I'll sort thru the stuff in here; we're going to have to get rid of the wet carton. My god, there are a lot of paper cups and plates in here. What was Skip thinking?
Sally (having joined the boys outside): Skip wanted to be prepared for everything.
Tim and Sally pitch-in and transfer the material out of the wet carton to a dry carton.
SD: Fred, I'm finished here, let's go eat.
Fred (putting the plastic trash bag down on the dock): Sounds like a great idea. Sally, coming to eat?
Sally: Yea, I'll join you, Skip is sleeping right now.
(As they are walking up the dock)
Sally: Did anyone find the showers?
SD: Yes, go up to the restaurant; do you remember where we exited out of the restaurant?
Sally: Yes.
SD: At that location make a left instead of a right and the ramp around to the shower is on your right. It's hidden between the buildings.
Sally: Is there a door combination?
SD: Yes, it took me about 3 minutes to open that door; I left it propped open.
Sally: You broke in?
SD: No, there are only so many combinations for five buttons. I kept trying.

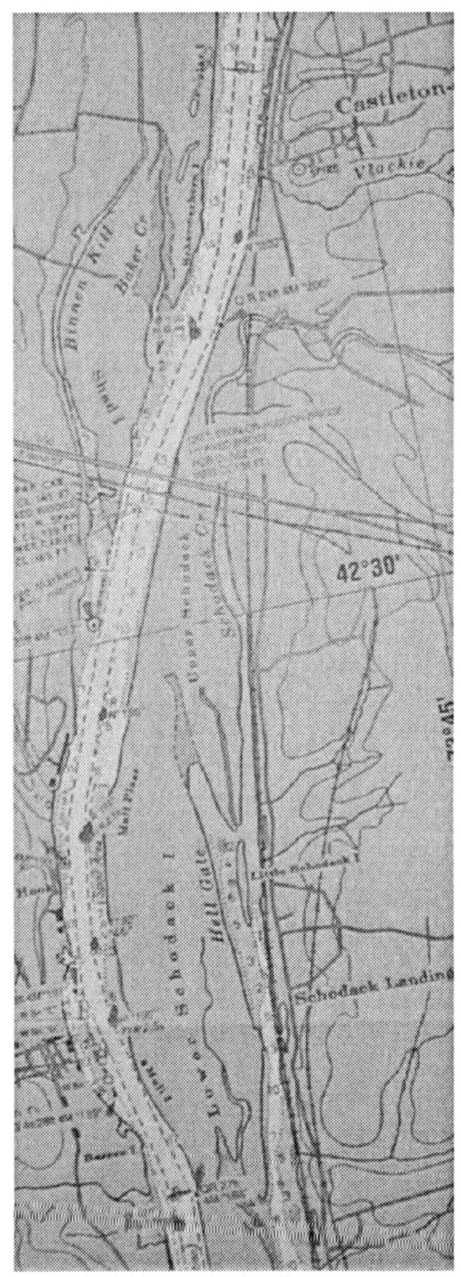

Stage 3 4.35 nautical miles.

Stage 4

Scene 1 Ghost of Lucky

Wednesday, August 17th, AM swim with a scheduled 5:00 am start. RoJo leaves from Coeymans and returns to Coeymans after the swim. Crew has lunch at Coeymans with Skip. Location—10 miles south of Albany, typical Hudson River scene with high tree covered banks. A deer is sighted in the water ahead of Skip. The scene opens with Tim and Sally on the bow of RoJo. Swim is underway having started at 5:50 am. Weather was foggy, flat water with a light breeze.
Sally: (blows whistle)
SD: Sally, you need to put a little more ump into that whistle.
Sally (sweetly): It hurts my ears.
Tim looks at Sally strangely.
Skip is heard swimming.
SD: Do you know how to do a stroke count?
Sally: No.
SD: Let me demonstrate. Every time his arms punch the water, it's considered a stroke and it gets a count. So you take a timepiece and maybe count for 15 seconds or 30 then multiply the number you count by 4 or 2 to get the strokes per minute.
Sally: Could you show me?
SD: Sure. Take my watch.
Sally: Okay.
SD: When it hits 15 we'll start. Let's do a 30 second count.
Sally: Now!
SD: One, two, three...
Tim counts up to 29 of Skip's strokes when Sally calls the ½ minute.
SD: twenty-eight, twenty-nine, thirty….
Sally: Stop.
SD: So he's doing about 60 strokes a minute
Sally: Seems easy enough.
Tim: With a watch, once you start, you can watch the sweep hand while you listen for the stroke.
(Later)
Sally does a count.
Sally: He's doing 62 strokes a minutes.
SD: That's typical of a guy. Men stroke around 56 to 66 strokes a minute. Girls go up to 80 strokes a minute.

Sally (boastfully): That's 'cause we're so good.
SD: Sally, on the log sheet it looks like there is a spot for the water temperature. Do we have a thermometer?
Sally (to Tim): I think Fred has an instrument he can get a reading on.
Sally (calling up to Fred): Fred, do you know the water temperature?
Fred: 82 degrees.
SD: My god it's warm. My wife wouldn't swim 2 miles in an eighty-degree pool; she'd be complaining that it's too hot. How does Skip do it?
Sally: I don't know.
SD: Sally, put down in the log that it's foggy.
Sally: Where does fog come from?
SD: That means the water is warmer than the air temperature.
Later, off New Baltimore, an object is sighted in the water well ahead of Skip.
Fred (calls down from the flying bridge): What's that up ahead.
SD: Looks like a crocodile.
Fred: Maybe it's a dog.
SD: It's the ghost of Lucky.
Sally: It's a deer.
Fred: You're right.
SD: Let's go have a closer look.
(Boat moves off from Skip)
SD: It's a deer all right.
SD: You know this deer is between jurisdictions. Open season!
Fred: I've never seen a deer swimming before but mammals do swim.
Sally: I've read that this is how Lyme disease got to Long Island.
SD: Interesting. In my book on swimming, I have records of horses falling into the East River when they were used in the eighteen hundreds as transportation. One horse swam all night after it fell in. I even found a report of an elephant swimming between Coney Island and Staten Island.
Fred: You're kidding.
SD: No, it was more recent, around 1970's or so. The animal escaped from a circus and wound up swimming to Staten Island.
Fred: Amazing.
SD: Where's Skip? Let's get back to him.

(Later)
SD: It looks like it's really foggy up ahead.
(Once in the fog bank)
Sally: Makes me feel isolated.
SD: Well, Fred has the radar on so he'll be able to detect tugs and barges.
(Later)
SD: Look how sunny it is here.
Sally: Love it.
Fred: We're coming up on Rattlesnake Island.
Sally (with distaste, on the bow): Rattlesnakes?
Fred: It's what they call it.
Sally (blows signal horn twice): That's it.
SD: Skip, you did over 5 miles.
SS: Great.

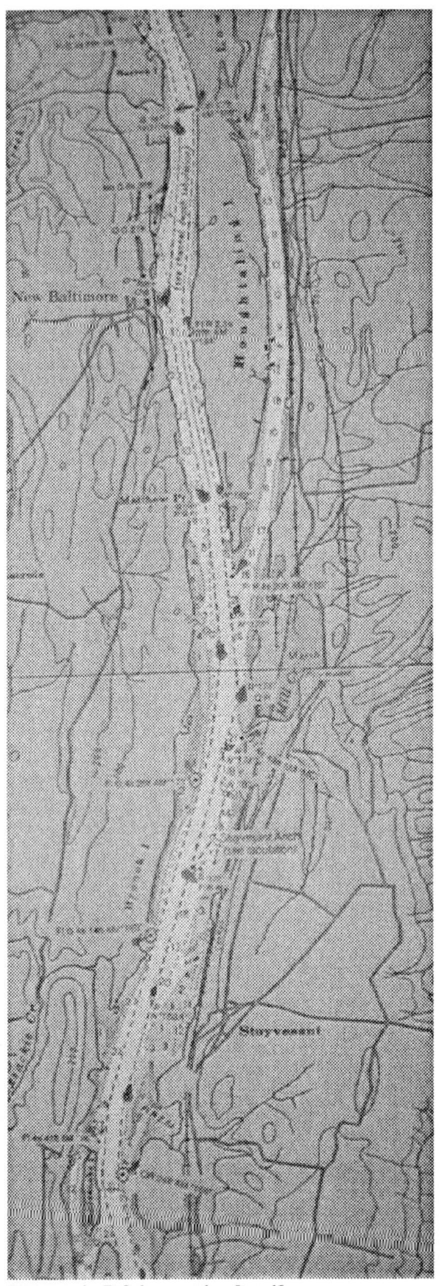

Stage 4 5.34 nautical miles.

Stage 5

Scene 1 Pretzel test

Wednesday, August 17th, PM swim with a schedule 4 pm swim start. Tim and Sally are in the dinghy for this swim. Scheduled start is off Rattlesnake Island. Weather is clear, calm and sunny. Start time is 4:43pm.

Fred: I got the motor for the dinghy back.

SD: Great, we'll get ready to launch.

Sally (looking thru the dinghy bucket): Is there a whistle in here? What are we going to do for a stopwatch? This one doesn't work. It stopped on me when I tested it.

SD: Let me see it. (Tim looks at it for a moment then tosses it overboard) Better to rely on anything else than have it mess up a swim.

Sally: That's great, now what am I going to use?

SD: Your cell phone. Mine has a stop watch feature.

Sally picks up her cell phone and starts looking at it pressing buttons.

SD: Fred, I need you to hold a position in the current so I can test it. You'll have to anchor.

Fred: You want me to anchor?

SD: Yup, drop anchor, I have to have a stationary object to test the current against.

(Later, after anchoring)

Fred: What's the idea?

SD: I have to test the current, it's been two days, four swims and we've only gone 16 miles. I might be putting him into the water too soon. I'm going to drop a pretzel stick at the front of the boat, let it float down the length of the boat, time it, and then calculate the current flow.

Fred: I can drop it up forward.

SD: Call it out and I'll use the stopwatch feature of my new cell phone.

Fred: Go

Tim sitting at the stern (after a pause): 28 seconds. This is not fast enough. Let me break out my calculator to see what it is doing (another pause while he calculates)

SD (muttering): 30 feet divided by 28 seconds is approximately one foot per second. Times sixty to get the number of feet per minute; then divided by 100 to find out the speed in knots. The

current speed is six-tenths a knot. Not fast enough to put Skip in. The rated top speed for this section is 1.7 knots. We'll test again in a half an hour after the current has built up.
(Standing on the back of RoJo, Tim and Skip discuss their planning)
SS: Tim, let's pick out some visuals for me.
SD: The water is deepest over on the left side of the channel for this stage.
SS: So we'll head for the red buoy. How about later on?
SD: I'd like you over by the eastern shore down here (point to the chart).
SS: I remember the last time I swam this we did real well along the shore of the Rip Van Wrinkle Bridge.
SD: Well, we might get there but we'll see.
SS: Let me show you where I predict I'll finish: Middle Ground Flats.
SD: Interesting. I hope we make it there.
SD (to Sally): I'm going to have to put sunscreen on before we head out.
(Later, Fred and Tim are testing the current; Fred has a pretzel in his hands)
Fred: Go.
SD: 11 seconds. Let's see (calculating) that's one point six knots. Time to get Skip in the water!
(Later, Skip is standing on the swim platform of RoJo after Tim and Sally cast off in the dinghy)
SS: Which way?
SD: Swim to the red buoy.
(Skip enters the water)

Scene 2 The tugboat tease
Scene opens with SD and Sally aboard the dinghy.
SD (to Sally): I wonder what's going on. We discussed the course before we left.
Sally (blowing signal horn): Ready, Go!
(The dinghy moves off from RoJo as it's still at anchor. About ten minutes later, RoJo joins the chase)
(Bit later)
Tim (on VHF): Fred, sorry about leaving you alone to pull the anchor.

Fred (on VHF): It was a trick but I got it done. I actually put the boat under way.
SD (on VHF): Really.
Fred (on VHF): I had to run down to the bow but I got it.
(½ hour after the start)
Sally (blowing the signal horn): What's the distance?
SD: One point three miles.
Sally: Tim, how many people have swum the Hudson?
SD: I could only find records for about a dozen. About every ten, twelve or so years, someone gets it into their head to swim the Hudson.
Sally: Why do you think so few have swum it?
SD: Well, the length of time to finish the swim and it takes a lot of organization to pull it off.
Sally (glancing forward): What's up ahead?
SD (pulling out the chart and laying it out on the bench seat): Let me check the chart.
SD: It looks like this is Middle Grounds Flat. The channel is off to the left. The water to the right is…tricky.
SS: Which way?
SD and Sally (not in unison, Tim first): Left, go left. It's too shallow a channel to the right.
SD: It'd be a great problem to solve, would it be quicker going across the shallows west of Middle Ground Flats for a swimmer or taking the current driven channel? We probably couldn't take the RoJo, as the depth is 3 foot in places. It sure looks like it's quicker that way; a straight shot down to the bridge.
Sally: We'll never know.
(½ hour later)
Sally (blowing the signal horn): Distance?
SD: Two point seven miles. This is great; he went further in the second half hour than in the first. The current picked up just like we planned.
Sally: There is a plan?
SD: Yes, we're dropping Skip in the water just before peak and that means his speed will pick up before it starts dropping.
SD (Tim stands up in the dinghy): I've got to stretch out.
Tim holds the motor control in one hand as he stands up. He notices something ahead looking like a log.
SD: Sally, do you see that up on the left?

Sally: Yes. Any idea what it is?
SD: No, but we might need the net. Have Skip swim to the right.
Sally (peering closely): It looks like a pile of eelgrass all clumped together.
(Later)
Fred (on VHF): Moran tug, Moran Tug, this is the RoJo.
Tug (on VHF): RoJo, this is the Margaret Moran. Switch to channel thirteen.
Fred (on VHF): Switching.
Fred (on VHF): Margaret Moran, this is RoJo. I'm the cabin cruiser ahead of you. We're escorting a swimmer down the Hudson. Is one bell all right?
Tug (on VHF): Yes, we've heard about him. We're okay with one bell.
Fred (on VHF): Can I get a slow bell?
Tug (on VHF): You sound like you know what you're doing.
Fred (on VHF): A long time ago I worked on the Eugene F. Moran. Is she still around?
Tug (on VHF): Now you're dating yourself. I don't believe she's working anymore.
Fred (on VHF): It was a long time ago.
Fred (on VHF): Dinghy escort, Dinghy escort, the northbound tug is asking us to stay to the green side of the channel.
SD (on VHF): We can do that; we're over there now so we'll just stay here.
Fred (on VHF): Sally, the boys on the tug are wondering if you could flash them.
Sally (to Tim): Give me that radio!
Sally (on VHF): What have you been telling them? No way!
Fred (on VHF): Please, it'd really help them out.
Sally has an awkward moment then her face lights up.
Sally (on VHF): Watch this.
Sally stands up on, stretches then bends over the bow and wiggles her tush in the air. She takes off her sweat suit top off seductively and then her sweat pants. Wearing her swim suit, she wiggles a bit more then sits down.
Fred (on VHF): Woo-woo.
SS (while swimming): Va-va-voom!
SD (in shocked disbelief on VHF): I think that's the show.
Tug (on VHF): I hope he beats the dog.

(Later)
Sally (after blowing the whistle): What town is that up ahead?
SD: I think its Hudson.
SD (gazing at the western shore): Sunset is coming up.
Sally: It's lovely.
SD: How much longer 'til the finish?
Sally: This is the second hour coming up.
SD: Oh, thank God. I'm stiff from sitting on this dinghy.
Sally (blowing the signal horn twice): Finished.
SD (on VHF): Fred, you can pick him up.
Fred (on VHF): I'll move closer.
SD (on VHF): Fred, where are we staying tonight?
Fred (emphatically on VHF): We're going to the Catskill Marina. It's a lovely place.
Sally: Where's that?
SD (to Sally): Somehow I suspect it's in the Catskills.

Stage 5 5.9 nautical miles.

Stage 6

Scene 1 Pre-swim preparation

Thursday, August 18th, AM swim with a schedule 5 am start. RoJo docks at the Catskill marina. The start location is off Middle Ground Flats. Weather is clear and calm. Scene opens on the stern of RoJo on the Hudson River just before 5:13 am start.

SD (to Fred): The start times are getting a little easier.

Fred: Six am is better than 4 am. Why the change?

SD: As we go down the Hudson, the tides will occur later and the daily progression moves the time slightly every day.

SD (reading the GPS then calling up to the bridge): Fred, this looks like the spot. We stopped last night just north of the green buoy #139; could you anchor again?

Fred: Only if you help me weight anchor.

SD: Will do.

SD goes below to help make ready for the swim.

SD: Skip, I was wondering how you are handling the warm water?

SS: I didn't bulk up for the swim. I knew it was only a couple of hours swimming a day and it would be warm. Don't forget, I swam the Hudson in eighty-eight. This isn't the English Channel.

SD: That's for sure.

SS: I'm looking at making the Van Wrinkle Bridge today.

SD: We've got a great current today for the swim.

SS: Do you want me in now?

SD: Let me check first. By the way, you were right on about the location last night.

SS: Oh, Middle Ground; hey, do I know this river or do I know this river?

(Sally drops a pretzel and Tim times it)

SD: 13 seconds. Now is as good a time as any, Skip.

SD (pulling in the line): Sally, let get the dinghy going.

Sally: I'm right behind you. Do we have another Gatorade around?

SD: There might be one left in the cooler from the last swim.

SD (to Fred): I'll go forward to pull the anchor.

(SD assists Fred weight anchor)

Fred: Just lay the line out on the deck.

Scene 2 Rip Van Wrinkle Bridge

(Later, SD and Sally are aboard the dinghy waiting for Skip to drift down to the start)
SD: All right, this is a good position. We could start him now.
Sally: Ready, Go. (Sound signal horn)
After five minutes
Sally: This is the five minutes.
Sally (blows whistle): Distance?
SD: Point two nine. Let's see, times twelve that means he'll be doing around three point six miles at the one-hour mark. We'll have to see if this early speed holds.
SD: The current should bring us close to the city of Hudson. We'll keep him headed for the mountain just off to the right of the city.
(Later)
SD: We're getting some good numbers going by Hudson.
Sally: What's he reading?
SD: Three point two knots.
(Later)
Sally: That's an interesting lighthouse here on the river.
SD (peering at the chart): I don't think it's occupied. The chart doesn't give a name for it. Could be the Athens, Hudson or even Middle Ground Lighthouse.
(Later)
SD (to Sally): I'm going to move him toward the center of the river. The river bends left up ahead and he'll want to be on the outside edge of it.
SS: Which way?
SD (looking ahead): Head for the chimney
SS: Which one?
SD: The tall one.
Sally: There's something up ahead in the water.
SD (staring ahead): Yes, odd looking.
Sally: There a lot of eelgrass around it.
SD: Let's try and guide him through, having him go left.
Sally: There's too much of it, there's no clear path
SD: He'll have to swim through it.
Skip shakes some eelgrass off his shoulders making some splashes.

Sally: That must have been a surprise for him.
SD: You know he looked like a Rastafarian with the eelgrass drape all over his head and shoulders there.
Sally: What are those dark things in the water with the eelgrass?
SD: I don't know. (a pause in the conversation occurs as they drift by some eelgrass) They are the size of walnuts. Let's fish one out of the water.
Sally and Tim retrieve a pod from the river.
Sally: That's the ugliest seedpod I've ever seen.
SD: You know, when I was a kid growing up in Southern California, we had sticker weeds that could make a child's life miserable. These look like they are sticker weeds for elephants.
(Later)
Sally: Do you know many swimmers?
SD: Yes, tons.
Sally: Who was the most unusual swimmer?
SD: There as one fellow back in the 30's named Zimmy who swam the entire length without getting out of the water.
Sally: Oh, my, gosh. How long did it take him?
SD: I think it was around 145 hours. He had an advantage over other swimmers: he was legless. So he could sleep in the water.
Sally: Yeah, but 145 hours, he must have been a wrinkled prune.
SD: That's for sure.
Later, under the Rip Van Wrinkle Bridge,
SD: He's doing 3.6 knots. This is huge.
Sally: Wow.
SD: It looks like Skip is going to get a squirt off the bend in the Hudson to go around Catskill Creek. We just have to keep him out of this little cove here (pointing off to the side).
Sally (brushing Tim's hand down): Tim, don't point.
Sally: Should I signal him to swim to the boat?
SD: Yes, I don't want him swimming into an eddy.
Sally: For sure!
SD (stands up to stretch out): Stretch time.
Sally stands up and does some yoga stretches including bending over. Her phone falls out of her pocket at one point into the water.
Sally: I dropped my phone!
SD: What luck.
(Sally sits down)

SD: Oh, these are big numbers, he's cranking going by the entrance to Catskill Creek. I can't believe it. How much time is left?
Sally: I don't know because my cell phone was tracking the time.
SD: Oh, here use my phone; they are all tied to the same clock.
Sally: There is about 3 minutes left in the swim.
Sally (blowing the signal horn)
SD: Skip, you were doing over 3.3 knots!
SS (stops swimming): Should I keep going?
SD (after thinking): No.
SS: Great job everyone!

Scene 3 DEC conversation
Scene at the dock in Catskill where Skip, Fred and Tim meet.
SD: I'm going to go see the dock master.
SS: Where's Sally?
SD: She's taking a walk to the Verizon phone store in town.
SS: What happened?
SD: Her phone fell in the water.
SS: That's the second phone this swim.
Fred: Do you know where there's a place to eat?
SD: Yes, Sally and I went to a nice breakfast place; in fact, it was called Nora's Nook around the corner, it's not far.
Fred: How do you get there?
SD: Go out the main gate, turn right, go up the hill to the boulevard and turn left. The restaurant is on your right about a block down. I'll catch up with you two there.
The three split up and Tim walks over to the Marina office holding a plastic bag.
SD: I was looking for someone that might know something about the eelgrass we've coming upon in the river.
Dockboy: There a Department of Environmental Conservation launch about two boats down from yours.
SD: Great, I'll wander over.
Tim walks down to the DEC boat.
SD: Hi, I'm wondering if either of you might know something about the marine fauna we've been coming across in the Hudson.
Doug: I'm pretty familiar with the fauna. What's your question?
Tim pulls the seedpod from a plastic bag he's been carrying around.

SD: What is this?
Doug: That's a water chestnut seed. It's an invasive specie that was brought to Lake Collins near Schenectady, New York which is northwest of Albany. Lake Collins is connected to the Hudson by the Mohawk River. The plant was nearly irradiated in the 1970's; we were down to hand pulling the few remaining plants when the money ran out.
SD: Well, this seed gets tangled up with the eelgrass and it makes it hazardous for swimming.
Doug: It's actually worse at a beach because it is a rooted aquatic. The seed sinks to the bottom then embeds itself in the sand where the plant grows.
SD: My god, that's not good for public swimming.
Doug: Are you with the swimmer trying to set the record swimming to New York City?
SD: Yes.
Doug: Well, I have some good news for you. You won't see this plant below Kingston because it only survives in water that's less than thirty parts per thousand salinity. Below the Kingston Poughkeepsie area the water is too salty.
SD: Thank you for your assistance.
Doug: My pleasure and good luck in the swim.
Tim walks uptown and joins Fred and Skip at breakfast
SD: Skip, I bumped into a naturalist for the DEP.
SS: Have we violated a rule? I haven't been urinating in the Hudson.
SD (chuckling): No, I was asking him about those plants we've been running into.
Fred: They originate from a pond by Kingston. You'll see it when we go into the next marina.
SS: One of those things poked me in the forehead when I was swimming.
SD: Well, I was asking him about those gigantic seedpods. They are water chestnuts and he said that below Newburgh we wouldn't see them anymore because of the salinity.
SS: That's good news. The eelgrass was there the last time I swam it so I'm use to it. It's not a problem.
SD: Okay.
SS: Come to think of it, the last time there were telephone poles in the water and tree limbs.

SD: You might have had an exceptional high tide that lifted the debris off the high water line. So far, it's been fairly clean. We've only seen a few items that we've moved you around and they've been limited in size.

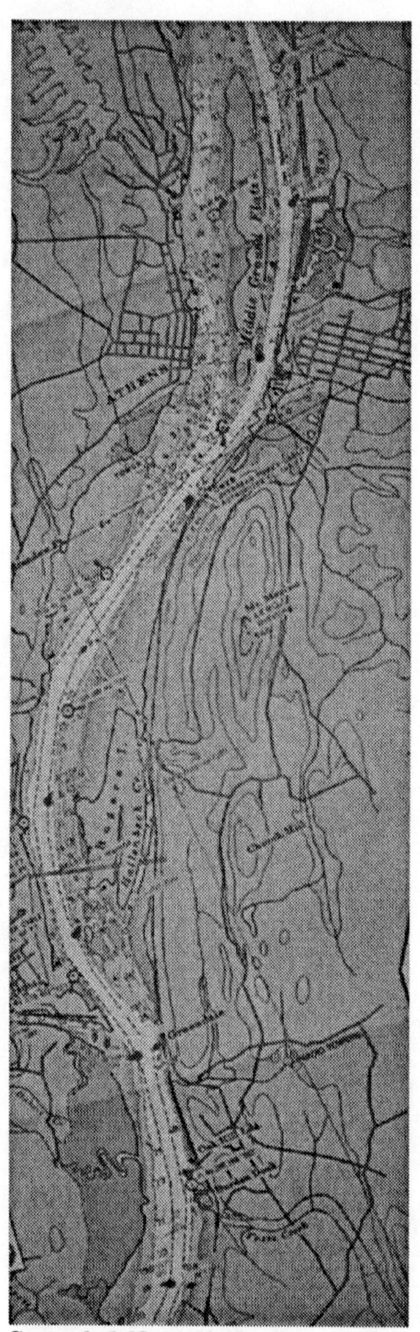

Stage 6 6.65 nautical miles.

Stage 7

Scene 1 Art, death, Olympics, and kayaks

Thursday, August 18th, PM swim, leave from Catskill marina and returns.

The afternoon swim picks up where it left off in the morning near a tree overhanging the Hudson River about a mile south of Catskill Creek. SD and Sally are in the dinghy. Weather is clear and sunny. Five pm start time.

SD: Sally, do you recognize this location?

Sally: No.

SD: I could have sworn we were located by a tree that looked like a weeping willow but wasn't. Now that we are here, the tree looks different from this morning.

Sally: I can't tell.

SD (looking at the GPS): This is the spot. Let's get Skip in the water.

Sally: Signals by hand for Skip to enter the water.

Sally (dropping hand to signal a start): Go!

SD: Somewhere around here is a home once own by a landscape artist.

Sally: Too bad the charts don't include tour information.

SD: The wife and I visited it and out of every window was a beautiful vista. The window really framed the scene. It was a very impressive site.

Sally: How so?

SD: The artist home was very eclectic. It had a whole room just for Chinese art. He also had a stage in another room.

Sally: Wow.

SD: He worked during the beginning of the era of photography so to make his work special he used very large canvases. His paintings are very dramatic with red, blue and green coloring featuring canyons and river valleys much like the Hudson River.

Sally: I've got a whistle coming up.

Sally stares intently at the watch and then blows the whistle.

SD: I remembered the name, Frederick Church. The home is called Olana.

Sally: Oh ugh, he's swimming by a dead fish.

SD: That's nothing, one year we found a dead body in the Manhattan Marathon.

Sally: Gross!

SD: Yes, it was just floating along, a swimmer nearly ran into it or at least that's what he claimed.
Sally: What happened?
SD: We started making up jokes about floaters.
Sally: No, silly, to the dead person.
SD: Oh, the harbor police fished the body out. I never saw it.
(Later)
SD: The River is quite wide here, I'm going to motor over to the green buoy side and see if there's a better current.
(Short trip away from Skip)
Sally: What do you think?
SD: Hard to tell. We'll move him over on the chance it's faster.
Sally: Let's get back.
SD: Moving.
(Back alongside Skip)
SD (answering cell phone): Hello.
ST (on the phone is a woman with an Australian accent): Tim, this is Shelley.
SD: Shelley, what's up?
ST: Tim, we're going to the Olympics!
SD: What?
ST: Open water swimming is going to be an Olympic sport.
SD: That's new. I'm actually on a swim right now.
ST: Where?
SD: Down the Hudson River. I'm in the dinghy alongside Skip Storch.
ST: You're so lucky; it's winter right now here in Australia.
SD (to Sally): Sally, see if we can bring him back along the dinghy.
(Sally hand signals Skip)
ST: Tim, I'm so excited, I've been crying for an hour.
SD: Shelley. You've been working on this for so long. This is great. Congratulations.
ST: Thanks, Tim. The distance is 10 kilometers and will be in 2008 at Beijing.
SD: Shelley, this isn't the first open-water swim in the Olympics. At the first Olympics, 1896, the swimming events were held offshore in a gulf. The distance event was 1200 meters.
ST: Tim, I should read your book.

SD: That's why I wrote it. You should say: open-water swimming is back.
ST: I'll do that. Tell Skip I wish him luck. I gotta go, bye.
SD (on cell phone): Bye.
Sally: Welcome back to the swim.
SD (to Sally): One of my swimming friends.
Sally: Who was she?
SD: Shelley Taylor-Smith. She's won the Manhattan marathon 5 times and she's secretary for the FINA open-water committee.
(Later)
SD: This section of the river is supposed to have a big current. I'm just not seeing it.
Sally: Here's some more eelgrass.
SD: Let's try and take him around it.
Sally: It's too wide a swatch.
SD: Signal him as best you can. Stand up; you'll get a better view.
Sally stands up and alternates signaling Skip to swim left or right.
The dinghy motor stalls out. Tim stares at the motor then lifts it to the stored position to clear the eelgrass off the propeller. He drops the motor back in and starts it.
SD: That was pretty thick eelgrass.
(Later)
SD: The bend in the river at Silver Point is coming up where we might pick up some speed. We'll put Skip along the shore.
(Later, going by a bulk cargo ship tied up at Silver Point cement plant)
SD (looking at the GPS): All right, here's the current, finally. He's over 3 knots. Nice.
(A few minutes later)
SD: That didn't last long. He's dropped below 3. How much longer?
Sally: About 10 minutes.
(Later)
SD (on VHF): Fred, can you get a photo of that house off Eves Pt?
Fred (on VHF): The one with the gazebo on the pier?
SD (on VHF): Yes.
(Later)

SD: Looks like some kayaks are on an outing.
Kayaker (paddling north): Hi, what's the event?
Sally: He's swimming to Manhattan from Albany.
Kayaker: Oh, we have a paddle every year over the same distance.
SD: Really, sorry I can't stay and talk, I have to stay with the swimmer.
Sally: There are quite a few of them. Why are they paddling against the current?
SD: You'd think they'd be paddling southbound but since they only draw an inch or two of water, it's not hard to stoke against the current.
(Later)
SD: Would you look at that: a private boathouse on the Hudson River!
Sally (blows signal horn twice, calls out): Skip, that's it.
SD (to Sally): It'll be easy to find the starting location tomorrow morning.
SD (calling out to Skip and pumping his fist): About six and a half miles tonight, Skip.

Scene 2 Dinner in Catskill

Fred, Sally, and Tim go to dinner at the restaurant in Catskill marina.
Fred: this restaurant is quite nice.
SD: Looks like a first class place.
Sally: Hostess around?
SD: Here she is.
Fred: Table for three.
Seated at the table with a view out the window of the creek the three, team members peruse the menu. Tim and Fred sit opposite Sally. Candlelight is low as is the music in the background with no other diners about.
SD: Waitress, while you're getting the drinks could we have a to-go order? We've another member of the team on the boat that is resting up.
Waitress: Is that the swimmer?
SD: Yes, he'd like a Cheeseburger.
Waitress: I'll get right on it.
Sally: What you getting Tim?

SD: I think I'm going with the surf and turf; I'm starved.
Sally: I might do the chicken marsala.
Waitress: Here's the take out.
Sally: I'll take it to Skip, can you order for me.
Fred: Sure.
Waitress: And your order?
Fred: I think I'll have the chili.
SD: Fred, you're not going to order chili. Please. I just couldn't handle it.
Fred: I like chili.
SD: Please don't order the chili. We're sleeping in the vee-berth.
Fred (to waitress): How's the chili?
Waitress: They have melted cheese over it. It's quite special.
Fred: Fine, that's for me.
SD (collapsing across the table): Oh, heaven help me. I'm going to die.
Sally returns.
Waitress brings dinner.
SD: Before I forget, the start time tomorrow morning is five forty-five am. We can sleep in.
Fred: I wanted to announce new sleeping arrangements.
Tim and Sally look at Fred in curious anticipation.
Fred: Tim's going to sleep in the salon with Skip and Sally is going to sleep with me in the quarter berth.
Sally: Surely you jest.
Fred: Nope, that's the way it's going to be.
SD: I don't even want to think about it. If I don't think about it, I won't have to go to confession.
Sally: Nothing going to go on.
Fred: Good. I'm exhausted and will most like be asleep by the time you get down there.
Sally: Did you get my order in?
Fred: Yes we did.
(The waitress brings the order)
Sally: What did you order?
Fred: Chili.
SD: Sally, I pleaded with him not to order chili.
Sally: This is unfair.
SD: Don't look at me.
Fred (spooning it down): Oh, this is good.

(Bit later)
Fred: I'm going to head back. See you tomorrow morning.
Fred leaves. Sally and Tim continue with their meal.
Sally: This would really be a romantic spot with the right person.
SD: I just hope we're not thinking about the same person.
Sally: Not likely.
Waitress (stopping by inquires): How's the food?
SD: The steak is too big, there are too many shrimp on my plate and the garlic potatoes are to die for. Other than that, it's okay.
Sally: The chicken is superb.
Waitress: Thank you!
(Later)
(The chief, a young lady, comes out)
Chief: How is everything?
SD: It's absolutely wonderful.
Chief: Thank you.
Sally takes a look at the chief and says nothing.
Sally (leans over and whispers): Did you see her? She's gorgeous.
SD: Who?
Sally: The chief.
SD: I didn't notice.
(Short time later)
Chief walks by returning to the kitchen; Sally drops her head and doesn't look up. SD smiles at the chief, glances at Sally then looked back and forth between the two.
SD: You're really taken with her?
Sally: I've been around men too long. I need to see some women.
SD: Don't we all.

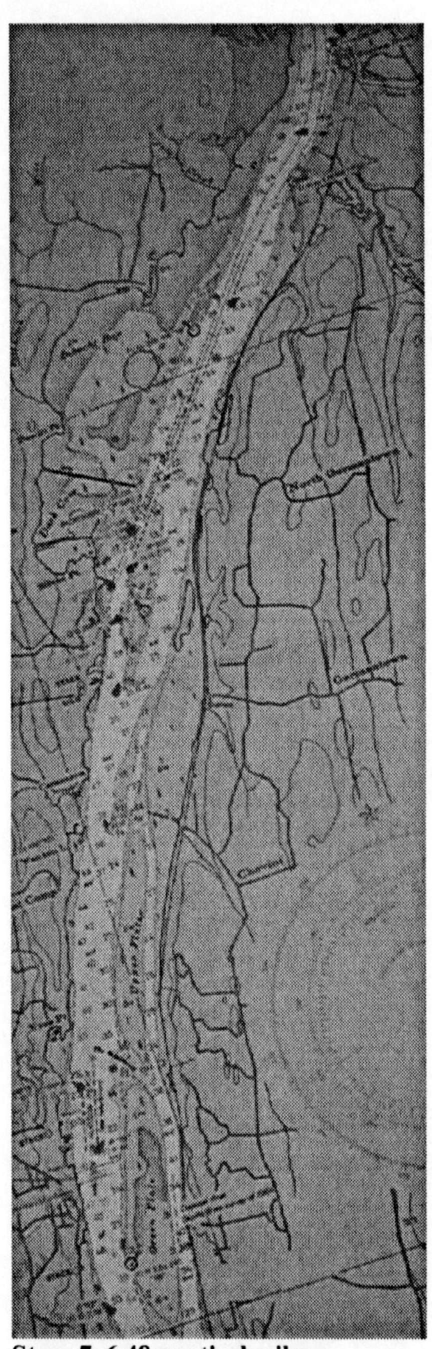

Stage 7 6.48 nautical miles.

Stage 8

Scene 1 Pre-swim planning

Friday, August 19th, AM swim. Leave Catskill and go to Saugerties Marina. Start location: Off Malden-on-Hudson. Weather: Clear, slight wind out of south. Tim and Skip in pre-swim planning aboard the RoJo just after 5:30 am while in route to the start.

SD: Skip, after this morning's swim, the current speed drops below 2 knots for the next few stages.

SS: Today's a great current then.

SD: We should make as good a use of this current as we can while it's here.

SS: How?

SD: I was thinking of keeping you in the water past 2 hours provided you are up to swimming longer. Last night I wanted to keep you in but didn't want to over stress you.

SS: I could do that. I'm feeling strong and this double workout is putting me in even better shape.

SD: What I'll do is use 3 knots as the criteria: if you are holding 3 knots at the 2 hours mark, I'd keep you in the water until it drops below 3 knots. If the pace is below 3 knots then there's no point in swimming any longer.

SS: We can use all the distance we can get while the current is good. I just don't want to go on and on in slow water.

SD: Would half an hour be too much?

SS: Yes.

SD: 15 minutes?

SS: I don't know.

SD: How about 5 minutes?

SS: That I could do.

SD: It's a plan, Skip.

Scene 2 A long swim

Scene opens with the swim underway, Sally and SD in the dinghy.

Sally blows the whistle.

Sally: E-yew, is that the same fish as yesterday?

SD: I think so.

Sally: How could it pass us?

SD: When Skip gets out, the tide is still moving. The fish is just floating with the tide. When the tide is ebbing the Hudson flows south and when it is flooding the Hudson flows north.
Sally: So the eelgrass Skip swam through earlier is the same eelgrass Skip swam through yesterday.
SD: I think you're right on that account.
(Later)
SD: Have you been watching the sunrise?
Sally: Yes, it's quite exquisite with the rosy colors playing through the clouds.
SD: Well, there's an old sailors ditty that says: Red skies at night, sailors delight; red skies in the morning, sailor take warning.
Sally: What kind of warning.
SD: To expect rough weather.
(Later)
Sally: What's this I've heard about a dog swimming down the Hudson?
SD: I found this news article in the New York Times that said a dog swam down the Hudson in 44 hours.
Sally (in disbelief): How'd they get the dog to swim, did they drag a bone in the water?
SD: I don't know. The only thing we know is the swim took 22 days and the time was 44 hours.
Sally: That's hard to believe.
SD: It's a claim and we don't even know if it's true. It could be a fake story.
Sally (with a tint of sarcasm): What, in the Times? A fake story, surely you jest.
SD: But I figure that the dog swam two hours a day and he had to swim when the tide was strongest.
Sally: Isn't that what Skip is doing?
SD: Yes, we've adopted the dog's strategy.
Sally: I have to concentrate; the whistle is coming up.
Sally stares at the watch then blows the whistle.
Sally: What kind of dog was it?
SD: A German Shepard.
Sally: What was the dog's name?
SD: Lucky.
Sally: Lucky?

SD: Yup, I think I've discovered the source of that joke about the lost dog.
Sally: What joke?
SD: You know how people post missing dog notices? Well, this one describes the dog as: blind in one eye, missing a leg, and recently castrated. The punch line is that the dog's name is Lucky.
Sally: Oh, yes, I remember that joke.
SD: I think we can add another line, swam the Hudson River.
Sally (chuckling): Yeah. How about, "last seen swimming down the Hudson River".
SD (laughing): Even better.
(Later)
Sally: Look at that beach with all the cars.
SD: That might be the location where all those kayaks put in yesterday.
Sally: Say, Tim, if we don't know that the dog story is true, how do we know Skip's swimming two hours a day, well, four hours a day, will set a record?
SD: On paper, Skip has the potential to blow the record off the map.
Sally: How's he doing so far?
SD: It's so bad that I've had to throw out my earlier projections. I'm going on blind faith now.
SD holds his one free hand out over the water.
SD: I *believe* in the River.
Sally (in disbelief): Oh, great.
(Later)
SD (to Sally): Skip and I have been talking about extending the swimming time if the current is good. How do you think a swim longer than 2 hours will affect him?
Sally: He's been feeling good and his recovery time has been excellent. He could handle some longer swims.
SD: Okay, how has he been holding up?
Sally: His stroke is helping quite a bit to keep his body together. Instead of being exhausted at the end of his swims, he's been breathing deeper and bi-laterally to get more oxygen in.
(Bit later)
Sally: Two hours is coming up. Are we leaving him in?
SD: He's holding 3.1 knots, if he's up for it, yes.

Sally blows signal horn twice.
SD: Skip, keep stroking.
Skip puts his head down and resumes swimming.
(Later)
SD (to Sally): When he reaches the bridge, we'll call the swim; the current has dropped off. I'm seeing some two point eights on the GPS.
Sally: What bridge is this?
SD (looking at the chart): Let me check, it looks like it's the Rhinecliff Bridge.
Sally: How far are we from Albany?
SD: It's about 40 nautical miles.
Sally blows signal horn 3 times right under the bridge.
SD (to Skip in the water): Skip, 7.4 miles!
SS: Terrific. I felt good. How long did I swim?
SD: 2 hours and 20 minutes.

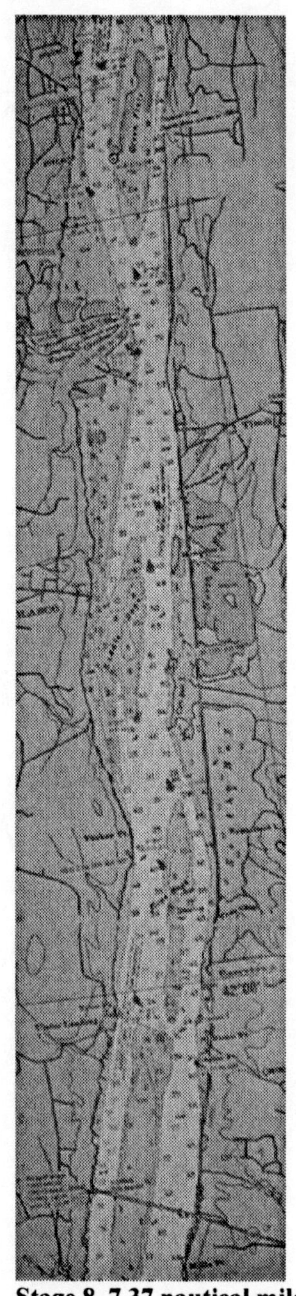

Stage 8 7.37 nautical miles.

Stage 9

Scene 1 A play is born

Friday, August 19th, PM swim. Leave Saugerties Marina for the swim and goes to Rondout Marina in Eddyville, the town on the south side of Rondout Creek from Kingston after the swim. We tie up next to the gas dock. Fred and his wife wanted to go to the wake for his friend's wife. Missed it due to relief boat failing to show. Fred hosts the swim on his boat. Magic Moment shows up during the swim. Sally's girlfriend shows up and they leave together for a motel. Kara arrives onboard after work. Weather: cool and overcast, storm threatens. Start time: 5:40pm. Scene opens on the stern of RoJo.

Fred (calls down from the flying bridge): Watch the towline, please.

SD: Sara, just check that you have drinks in the bag and can you find the tape for the tape machine?

Sally: Tim, I'm busy right now.

SD: Okay.

SD puts on his rain jacket. Sally is bundled up as well.

After the dinghy is launched, Skip takes a position on the swim platform and waits to be told when to jump in.

SD: Skip, in the water.

Skip: Now?

SD (nodding): Now, we're under the bridge.

SD: Sally, let's wait until he floats down to us.

Sally: He looks anxious to start swimming.

SD: All right, give him a start signal. He's close enough.

Sally: Ready, Go (blows the signal horn)

(After the start)

Sally: I can't wait for tonight. My girlfriend is coming tonight and I'm sleeping in a bed.

SD: Okay.

Sally: It's all about me, you know.

SD: (after a pause) Really?

Sally: Par-ty (waves her hands in the air, singing). My girlfriend is coming to see me tonight.

SD: Sally, you're not going to get all gushy and excited when she shows up are you?

Sally (sheepishly): No-o-o.

SD: Good.

(Later)
SD: This current is moving nicely. Let's head Skip up on the tip of the land by the lighthouse.
Sally (signaling): Closer to the boat?
SD: Yes.
SD: He's got the right course now. You could put your hand down.
Sally: Oh.
SD (staring off into the setting sun): I think I'm going to write a play about the swim.
Sally: Oh, go on.
SD: No, really.
Sally: How could you stage a play around someone swimming?
SD: Oh, the audience wouldn't see him; just the two people on the dinghy.
Sally: What would they talk about?
SD: What we have been talking about.
Sally (staring at Tim): What *have* we been talking about?
SD: Life! The river, the people, the experience are all part of this swim.
Sally: Life? For goodness sakes, Tim, we're only on a swim.
SD: Right and it's in our being in the moment and affirming our existence…
Sally: Tim, we're in a rubber raft in the middle of a river watching Skip swim.
SD: Yes. Look at all we've got: the river, the sunsets and sunrises, the quiet (Tim looks at the motor), the views. It's all ours. Skip's swimming and we're got all this around us.
Sally: And Skip has the eelgrass.
SD: Who would have thought that taking a rubber raft down the Hudson at 3 knots could be such a great vacation? It's so *gorgeous* and we're doing something that has a slight bit of importance to it.
Sally: It was pretty this morning.
SD: Sally, the last people to take a trip this slow down a river was Huck Finn and company.
Sally (excited): Oh, I wonder whose going to play me?
SD: I don't know.
Sally: I have to blow the horn, cover your ears.
Sally blows the whistle.

Sally: What's the distance?
SD: Its three quarters of a mile. That's pretty good for a quarter hour. Figure a mile and a half in a half hour, three miles in one hour and six miles in two.
Sally: We'll have to see if it comes true.
SD: Why should anyone have to play you?
Sally: I'm not an actor.
SD: Look, let's pretend we're re-enacting an updated version of *Life on the Mississippi*. You play Jim the escaped slave and I'll play Huck.
Sally: What are you talking about?
Huck (SD with a drawl): Jim, you know what I'm talking about.
Jim (Sally jumping in): No, Huck, I don't. I wish Tom were here. He's always kind to me.
Huck: Tom is here Jim, that's him swimming alongside the raft. Say, where'd you get that accent? Ain't you from the South?
Jim (staring): South Jersey is my home. How long has he been out there?
Huck: Never you mind about Tom. Now, Jim, there are slavers in Kingston that are probably looking for you.
Jim (frightened): Huck, this is awful. What am I going to do?
Huck: Jim, when we draw close to Kingston, I want you to jump into the river and hide on the far side of the raft.
Jim: Huck, I can't swim.
Huck: Tom can swim.
Jim: I ain't Tom.
Huck: Never said you were.
Jim: I guess you didn't…I still can't swim.
Huck: Don't have to.
Jim: Huck, you told me to jump in the river.
Huck: How else you going to duck down enough to hide behind the raft. Just don't let go of the raft.
Jim (smiling): Huck, I ain't never gonna let go of the raft.
Sally (checking her watch): Gotta blow this horn.
SD: I think the movie with that line is the *Horn Blows At Midnight*.
(Later)
Sally: So, what'd think?
SD (looking at the GPS): This is a real nice rip current here.
Sally: No, Tim, about my acting?

SD: Sally, I don't know anything about acting. Well, I'll take that back. You can always tell a good actor or director for that matter by turning down the volume on the TV and seeing if you can understand the emotion they are communicating. Acting 101.
Sally: What's that boat coming up ahead?
SD: That looks like it might be the replacement boat.
Sally: Better late than never.
SD: Let's hope they can get with the program. I know Fred had asked them to come up early to relieve him. Guess they couldn't make it.
(Later)
Sally: Final bell coming up! Are we leaving him in?
SD: No, he's dropped below 3 knots.
SD (on VHF): RoJo, RoJo, this is the dinghy.
Fred (on VHF): Go ahead.
SD (on VHF): We're going to be picking him up soon. Could you get in position for a pickup?
Fred (on VHF): Roger.
Sally blows the signal horn twice. Skip stops swimming.
Sally: That's it, Skip.
SS: Want me in longer?
SD: No, the current is dropping.

Scene 2 Dockside at Rondout marina
Later aboard the RoJo dockside. Sally and Kara are plummeting Skip various appendages. Her girlfriend sits quietly aside. SD enters to brief Skip on the stage and plan for AM swim.
SD: Kara, when did you get in?
Kara: About 15 minutes ago. I'll be here for the weekend; I have to work on Monday then I'll be back for Tuesday.
SD: Kara, okay, keep in contact as I don't know this moment where we'll be tomorrow much less on Tuesday.
Sally: Tim, this is Dolly, my girlfriend.
SD: Hello.
Dolly nods hello
SS: How'd I do?
SD: Only 5 and a quarter miles. The current dropped off. I may have started you too late.
Skip: That's not good.

SD: We didn't have a great current. It was rated at one point nine. That means you should have picked up nearly four miles just from the current. We're getting about 50% of the rated current.
Skip: Should I swim faster?
SD: No, just give me your regular pace. The current is going to be whatever it's going to be. If there was a one point nine ebb out there, we didn't find it.
Fred (from the galley): Tim, I won't be here tomorrow.
SD: I'm sorry you have to go; you've been a great help.
Fred: I'm quite please to meet everyone. I have to get back to my job and get the boat home.
SS: What's the start time tomorrow?
SD: I haven't figured it out yet. I'm going over to meet the new crew and brief them. I'll let everyone know as soon as I can.
Fred: Psst, his nickname is Corona Boy.
SD: Corona Boy?
Fred: Don't tell him that but you'll find out.
SD goes over to the new support boat *Magic Moment* to meet the crew.
SD: Gentlemen, I'm Tim Johnson
CP: I'm Captain Pickering and this is Ed, he's my mate.
Ed: Would you like a beer?
SD: No, I'm fine. I have to figure out what time we're starting the swim in the morning.
CP: Well, let's have seat at the table in the salon and look at the charts.
SD: Is there a place to plug in.
Ed: Should be.
SD, CP, and Ed sit down at the salon, Tim plugs in after some time then turns on his computer. CP and Ed drink and engage in idle chatter about the boat.
SD: All right, according to the tide program tomorrow's swim should begin about six am.
CP: Where will the start be?
SD: Should be right where we left off tonight, just south of the creek at Kingston.
CP: You know, we barely made it here tonight.
Ed: The starboard engine was apart until this morning.
CP: I've been putting motors and electronics together all day.

SD: How'd the boat run coming up here?
Ed: It was good.
CP: And what do you want us to do?
SD: Well, provide transportation to and from the starting locations then during the swims make a *Securité* announcement then standby to advise river traffic of our position and help figure out the currents.
CP: We're not going to make any announcements.
SD (surprised): Oh.
CP: You'll want Ed for the current.
Ed: My family summered at Catskill. Ever since I was a kid, rather than trailer our dinghy, I'd run up the Hudson to Catskill with two tanks of gas in a twelve foot outboard.
SD: Your parents would let you go by yourself?
Ed: Yup!
SD: You must have had a good time. I can certainly use someone with some knowledge of the current from that perspective.
CP: Ed, see if there is another Corona in the cooler.
Ed (opening the cooler): Looks like we're down to the last one.
CP: We're going to have to make a run.
CP moves over to the head.
CP: Let me show you how the head works. Hold this button in when you are flushing. No paper! I have a container that you should put the paper in.
CP goes in and uses the toilet. Tim works away on the computer and filling out the log sheets. A loud pounding is heard just before CP exits the head.
SD: What was that noise?
CP: I got tired of those hand pumps so I installed a reciprocating pump.
SD: For tomorrow morning, should we use Fred's dinghy or yours?
CP: We can use mine. It's all set up.
SD: I'll get the gear together and put it onboard tonight. The girls will probably be moving some of their stuff and the swimmer has quite a bit.
CP: What ever.
SD: Mind if I sleep here tonight?
Ed: The table folds down into a bed so it should work out.

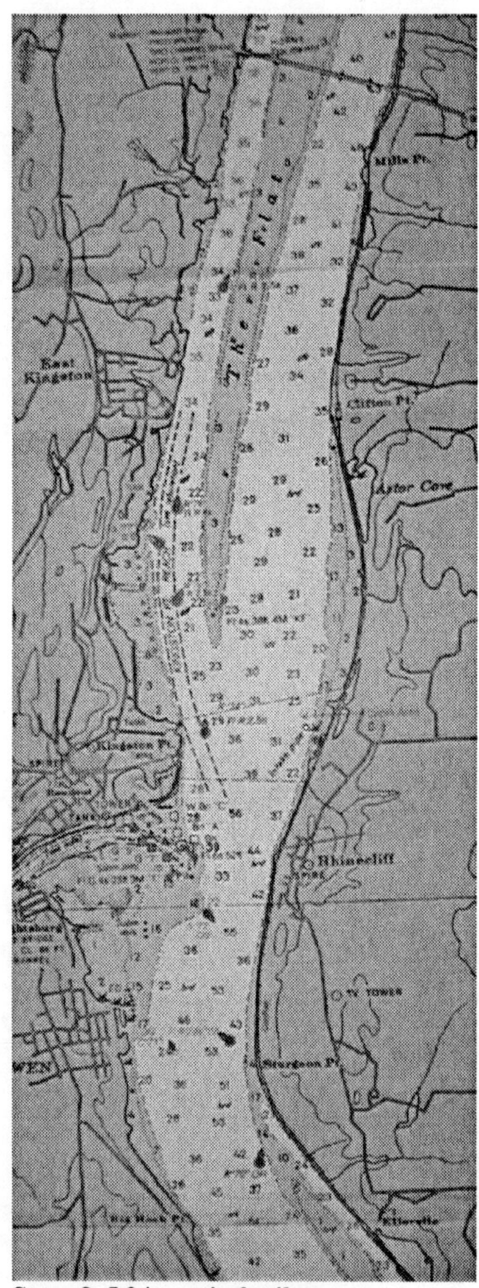

Stage 9 5.24 nautical miles.

Stage 10

Scene 1 Pre-swim preparation aboard the RoJo

Saturday, August 20th, AM swim. Start time: 6: 16 am.
Weather: clear skies, choppy water. Scene opens aboard Magic Moment at Rondout Marina before the swim start.
CP (putting his beer down): We'll keep the dinghy stored on the stern until we get to the starting location. Do you know where we're going?
SD: Yes, I do. Do you have a GPS?
CP: No, I've used Loran for a long time and just reinstalled it. It's not working. Remember, our starboard engine was overhauled just before the start of this trip.
SD: All right, let me get mine and turn it on. I'll be able to give you some directions to the waypoint.
After getting underway, Magic Moment pulls out into the Hudson from Rondout Creek and runs down to the starting location.
SD (to Ed who is at the helm): It's directly ahead about 500 yards, 300, 200. Okay, turn upstream and we'll get the dinghy and the swimmer in the water. Try and hold your position in the water.
Kara: What's the story?
SD: They are going to launch the dinghy; we'll put our equipment on it then go to the starting location. Skip will then start off the swim platform.
Kara: Do you have the swim log?
SD: Yes, it's in the bucket.
Kara: I'm going to put some of my drinks in the cooler.
Kara (opening the cooler): There's nothing but Corona beers in here. Where should I put our drinks?
SD: Let me check the cooler inside the cabin. I put some of our stuff in there last night.
Kara: If there's room, we can move some of these beers.
Ed (calling down from the flying bridge): You could hand one or two of those beer up here.

Scene 2 Swept away

Scene opens with SD and Kara on the water in the dinghy.
Kara: Are we ready?
SD: Yup, let's get Skip underway.

Kara (blowing signal horn): Go, Skip!
(Bit later)
Kara (blows whistle): Distance?
SD: Point two nine. That's a nice number for five minutes. Did you see the wake off the red buoy?
Kara: Yeah.
SD: We're looking at holding Skip in the current, which I believe will be right in the channel.
(A bit later)
SD: Kara, the motor is a Yamaha.
Kara (cautiously): Yes.
SD: Do you know what Yamaha means in Japanese?
Kara: No.
SD (chuckling): Johnson.
Kara sighs and goes back to watching the time.
(Later)
Kara (blowing signal horn): 15 minutes, what's the distance?
SD: Point six. Six tenths of a nautical mile in a quarter hour? Something's up. We've slowing down.
SD looks around for ½ second.
SD (on VHF): Magic Moment, what do you have for depth?
Ed (on VHF): I've got 13 feet.
SD (on VHF): Yikes, we've been swept out of the channel.
SD: Kara, signal Skip to swim away from the boat.
After SS responds
Kara: Is that okay?
SD: Have him turn more. We're going to have to make that red buoy up ahead.
SD (looking at chart): We're in a large eddy that's filling Vanderburgh Cove.
Kara: How'd we get there?
SD: We were on the edge of the channel and the current just moved us sideways. I should have picked up on it looking at the last red buoy.
Kara: How?
SD: The wake didn't go directly toward the next buoy in line but was cocked slightly toward shore.
SD (on VHF): Magic Moment, could you go over and check for the edge of the channel? Look for a depth change.
Magic Moment moves west in the river.

Ed (on VHF): I've got 24 feet over here.
SD (on VHF): You're about 100 feet further west than we are so we'll hold him on this angle until he breaks free of the eddy.
SD (to Kara): I want him to cross in front of that red buoy.
(Bit later the buoy goes by fairly close)
SD (on VHF): Magic Moment, how's our depth now?
Ed (on VHF): Twenty-four feet.
SD (on VHF): Good.
SD (to Kara): Kara, I'll turn the dinghy onto our new course, have him follow us.
After the maneuver,
SD: That was nearly perfect.
Kara: We're like synchronized swimmers.
Kara: 1st half hour coming up.
Kara (blowing signal horn): Distance?
SD: One point three. I think we lost five minutes and two tenths of a mile in that eddy.
(Later, Skip sees tiny Esopus Island)
SS (stopping): Which way?
SD: Right, go to your right.
SS: Can't hear you.
Kara (louder than Tim): Swim to your right.
Skip resumes swimming.
(Later)
Kara (frustrated): Oh, I missed the hour.
SD: What time is it now?
Kara: Sixty-two minutes.
SD: Blow the whistle anyway.
Kara (blows the signal horn): Distance?
SD: Two point four eight miles. Not particularly fast. That eddy really hurt us.
Kara: Let's do a cheer.
SD: What?
Kara (shout while standing up and raising her hands): Go, Skip.
SD (follows suit): Go, Skip.
Action repeats and Skip says…
SS (without stopping swimming): Cool.
(Later as they come along the western shore near Esopus)
Kara (pointing): There's a deer over by the water.
SD (looking): Where?

Kara: Just by that clearing.
SD: Oh yeah, I see it. I wonder if it is coming down to go swimming.
Kara: Yeah, right.
SD: Really, a few days ago we saw a deer swimming across the Hudson.
Kara (surprised): That must have been something.
Skip comes to the end of this stage just north of Hyde Park.
Kara (blowing signal horn twice): You're finished, Skip.
SD (on VHF): Magic Moment, Magic Moment. You could pick Skip up now.
Ed (on VHF): Our pleasure.
Kara: What's the distance?
SD: I'll have to give it to you later, I pushed the wrong button and the GPS is now reading the distance to the finish.

Scene 3 Laundry
That was our 1st swim with Magic Moment. Fred left his boat at Rondout for us to sleep on and is occupied by Skip. Tim switches dinghies before the swim. Eventually, the entire crew shows up for breakfast at the restaurant and sit on the veranda at Rondout Marina. CP and Ed are drinking Corona beers.

Scene opens at the dockside restaurant of Rondout Marina. SD is sitting with Skip and Andy. Sally shows up in the company of a different woman. SD goes to investigate.
SD: Sally, welcome back. Who's your friend?
Sally: This is Rosemary. She owns the Bed and Breakfast I stayed at last night.
SD closely and longingly reads the writing on Rosemary's shirt top. Rosemary is generously endowed.
SD: Rosemary, how nice to meet you. Is that song lyric by the Ronettes?
Rosemary: I think so.
SD: Are you down here often?
Rosemary: I actually own the gift shop.
SD: Oh. We were looking at purchasing some sweatshirts earlier.
Rosemary: Why don't I donate them to the swim?
SD: Okay. Have you met Skip?

Rosemary: No, but I have to get back, my boyfriend and I are meeting for lunch.
Rosemary walks off with Sally following close alongside.
SD returns to find CP and Ed have joined the breakfast group. Skip and Andy excuse themselves and leave.
SD: Ed, I'm sorry you missed that. Did you get a look at Rosemary?
Ed (with enthusiasm): Oh I didn't miss that; I had my binoculars out.
SD: My god, you're on top of everything.
Ed: I'd have liked to be on top of that.
SD: Don't you have a girlfriend?
Ed: Yes I do; but she's been on my case lately.
SD: Oh, it wouldn't be about drinking would it?
Ed (in amazement): Why yes it is, how'd you know?
SD: Lucky guess.
Later that afternoon, SD is sitting on the stern bench seat of Magic Moment.
CP (leaving the boat carrying his laundry): I'm going up to the laundry, got anything?
SD: Let's see, I've been on a boat for a week now. I've use one t-shirt, one pair of underwear, and a pair of socks and I've got spares of everything. Naw, I don't need the laundry.
Ed (holding a beer in his hand, speaking from the flying bridge): I can get two weeks out of underwear.
SD: How?
Ed: I turn them inside out and wear them for another week.
SD: You can turn them inside out? I never imagined.
CP: Then you can wear them backwards and get another two weeks out of them.
SD (laughing and falling down, gasping for breathe): Stop, stop, you're killing me.
CP: Then Ed sprays it with Glade and gets another four days out of 'em.
SD gasping for breath; loud guffaws are heard.
Kara: Glade?
Ed (embarrassed): You're not telling that story?
CP (taking a swallow on his beer, smiling and speaking to Kara): Yes, he did that. Got a little rash out of it too!

Scene 4 Revised plan

Later, after Skip wakes up from his afternoon nap SD joins him in the cabin aboard the RoJo.

Skip: How's everything going? Are we getting the current?

SD: Today was as bad as yesterday, only 5.2 miles. I don't know what's going on with the current. This river is not kicking like I had hoped.

Skip: What the impact on the swim?

SD: Remember that initial estimate I send you?

Skip: Yes.

SD: We're so far off track I've had to scratch out everything.

Skip: What are we going to do? Tim, I've sunk over $10,000 of my own money into this swim when I couldn't get a major sponsor.

SD: We need to a new plan. (Tim shows Skip the computer display) Looking ahead, we have what I'd call the doldrums; the best the current does is 1.6 or 1.7 knots until we reach the Tappan Zee Bridge. We need a minimum of 5 miles every swim out of you to make the finish and set the record.

SS: Where's the chart, let's check it out. Plot every swim assuming I make 5 miles a swim.

Skip and Tim measure out the remaining swims assuming 5 miles each stage on the chart. Tim lays it out then Skip double checks it.

SS: This puts us down at the Tappan Zee Bridge at 36 hours.

SD: Well, it puts us within striking range of the finish, about 2 miles north of the Tappan Zee Bridge. Below the Tappan Zee, it can be done in one swim; I'd estimate an 8-hour swim.

SS: I don't know if I could do an 8-hour swim at that point, I've only trained for 2 hour swims.

SD: Let's just see what happens over the next few days. We've got a lot of swimming to do. Every swim is crucial.

SS: I'll give it my best.

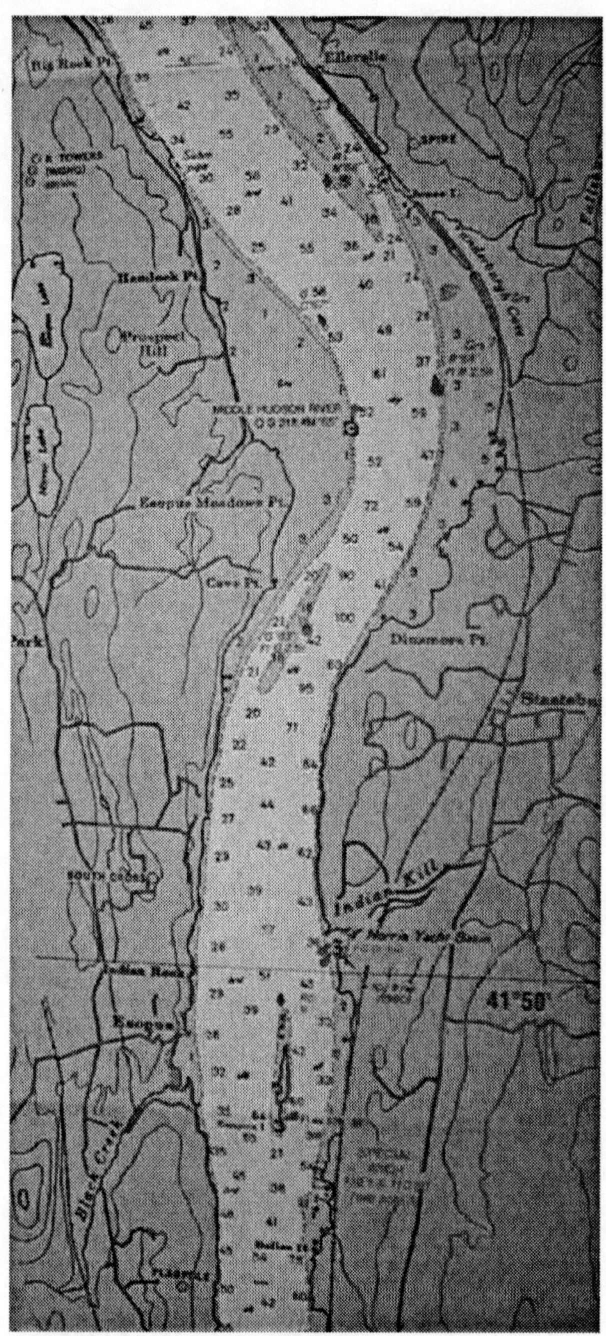

Stage 10 5.2 nautical miles.

Stage 11

Scene 1 Pre-swim preparations

Saturday, August 20th, PM swim. Starting time: 6:20 pm. Weather: 1-foot chop with 10 knot wind out of the south at the start; flat and calm at the end. The team leaves Rondout on Magic Moment and after the swim travels to Brass Anchor Restaurant marina.

Scene is aboard Magic Moment at the starting location off of Hyde Park.

SD (from the flying bridge of Magic Moment): Okay, we're close enough to drop the dinghy in the water.

Scene shifts to the stern of Magic Moment.

CP (goes to drop the dinghy, set up the motor, then load the equipment aboard): We're on it.

SD: Kara, are you going in the dinghy?

Kara: Yes.

SD: Bring a jacket as it looks like a front may come through. I'm wearing mine.

SD (to Brian): Do you have an old towel or something to put across the plywood seat of the dinghy? The edges are a little rough and I don't want to pick up a splinter.

CP (looking around and picking up an old worn towel): Try this.

SD puts on his rain gear.

CP: You have Atlantic foul weather gear?

SD: Yes, I'm going to have to replace it soon. It's worn out.

CP (returning from the cabin with his gear and a beer): Here is mine. I've had it 13 years.

CP displays a vintage set of raingear covered with plastic.

SD: That looks exactly like mine. Do you wear it?

CP: No.

CP turns and hangs the gear up in a closet. SD has a perplexed look.

Scene 2 Kara's interview and racing a tugboat

Scene opens on the dinghy from Magic Moment, SD and Kara aboard, Sally stays aboard Magic Moment with Skip.

SD (on VHF): Magic Moment, we've drifted downstream. I'll go back upstream to the drop location.

Ed: (on VHF): We'll follow you.

(Dinghy is repositioned about 200 yards upstream).

SD (on VHF): Okay, let's get Skip in the water.
(After Skip enters the water, he takes a few strokes then looks at us and waits for the whistle)
Kara (blowing signal horn): Ready, Set, Go!
SD: Wind is up a bit tonight.
Kara: Yes, it is.
SD: Kara, I've noticed you've mentioned that you're a physical therapist.
Kara: No. I'm a certified athletic trainer. An ATC.
SD: How does that differ from what Sally does?
Kara: She's a massage therapist and she would deal more with injuries.
SD: But you don't?
Kara: No, I don't see the same...(searching for the right word) diseased population. I'm keyed on athletes and the prevention, care, and management of sport injuries.
SD: Did you go to college for this?
Kara: Yes, at Ithaca. They're well known for education of athletic trainers.
SD: What would you take in the way of courses?
Kara: Anatomy, physiology, biology, kinesiology, (pausing to think) nutrition, and others along with the usual college level courses in English and other electives.
SD: Do you get any practical experience at Ithaca?
Kara: Just a minute, Tim. (Blows whistle) What's the distance?
SD: Half a mile. In ten minutes, not bad, he's hitting three knots all ready.
SD: How did you get your practical training?
Kara: Yes, we have a clinic where you are assigned hours plus I was assigned to the tennis team and the football team.
SD: What would you do?
Kara: I'd get them into saunas if they needed them or wrap injuries.
SD: Did you ever notice anyone who didn't think much of your abilities? You were just a student starting out?
Kara: One assistant coach blamed me for one of his players not making it on the field.
SD: That must have been difficult.
Kara: I tried to ignore it.
SD: What do you do for Skip?

Kara: I make sure he's stretched and warmed down from the swims.
(Later)
Kara (blowing the signal horn): This is the 1st hour. What's the distance?
SD: Two point eighty eight. I'm going to take my rain gear off; the weather seems to have died down. Here comes another barge.
(Later)
SD: Kara, we're going to leave him in until he reaches the bridge.
Kara: There's a freight train going over the bridge.
SD: It's sure moving slow.
Kara (blowing the signal horn): This is the 2nd hour.
SD (signals Skip to keep going): Distance is five point eighty-five.
SD: He'd be motivated to reach the bridge since he's been looking at it for the last hour or so.
Kara (as we reach the first bridge): Its two hours two minutes.
SD: Oh, look, there's another bridge just a ways down.
Skip stops swimming.
SD (pointing): Skip, go for the second bridge.
Skip resumes swimming.
Ed (on VHF): Tim, a southbound tug is behind us.
SD (on VHF): Got him in my sights Ed. He hasn't turned to line up on the bridge yet. We're going to try and make the second bridge.
Ed (on VHF): Just trying to make you aware of the limited room to maneuver under these bridges.
SD (on VHF): Thank you. I think we can beat the tug to the 2nd bridge.
SD is seen looking ahead at the bridge and then behind at the tug over and over. After a few minutes Skip reaches the 2nd bridge.
Kara (blowing the signal horn): That's it Skip.
SD (on VHF): Magic Moment, go ahead and pick him up.
Ed (on VHF): Tim, we'll get Skip but we'll pick you up over by shore.
Tim moves dinghy away and watch tug go by as Skip emerges from the Hudson.
SD: Kara, that was close.

Kara: Tim, I don't know what gets into you, sometimes.
SD: This was a great swim today. He went over a mile further than yesterday.
Kara: He also went over two hours.
SD: What's the official time?
Kara: Two hours twelve minutes.
SD: Wow, an extra mile in twelve minutes, gorgeous!

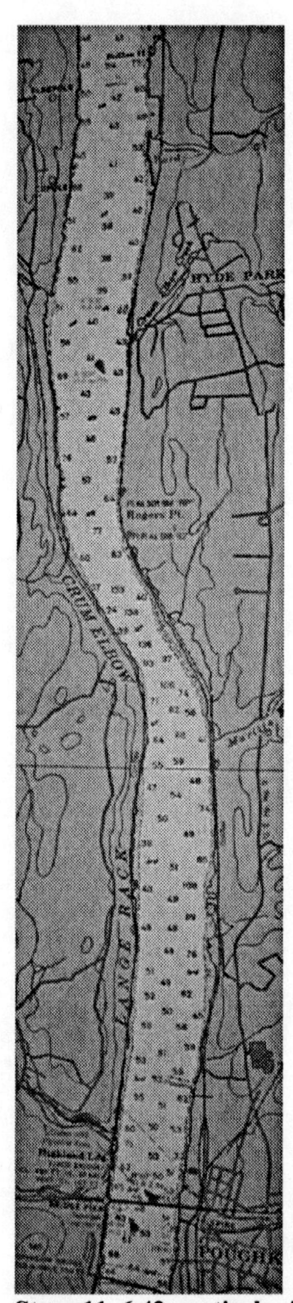

Stage 11 6.42 nautical miles.

Stage 12

Scene 1 Cement plant

Sunday, August 21tt, AM swim. Starting time: 6:20 am.
Weather: 1-foot chop was back, clear sky. Scene opens with SD and Kara aboard the dinghy with the swim underway, Mid Hudson Bridge receding in the distance.
SD: That was the Mid Hudson Bridge we started under.
Kara: I don't believe I've ever gone over it.
SD: Supposedly, there are Peregrine falcons nesting in the structure and one was reported to have attacked a woman jogger.
Kara: That must have been a surprise.
SD: Yes, I didn't see any menacing birds today.
Kara: I've heard there are eagles along the Hudson.
SD: I don't recall seeing anything like that but then again, I haven't been gazing up toward the sky that often.
(Later)
Kara: Skip seems to be swimming away from us.
SD: Signal him to come closer.
Kara: He's not coming over.
SD: All right, let me motor over there.
Kara (blowing signal horn): Distance?
SD: One point three six. Not too far but acceptable.
Kara: The speed picked up?
SD: Yes, it was below three oh and now it's reading three oh.
Kara (pointing): Look at that.
SD: Looks like a Blue Heron. Your horn must have disturbed it.
(Later)
SD (on VHF): Does anyone know what this plant is coming up on our left?
Red (Red Grenier, owner of Sunset on the VHF): That's the Buchanan cement plant.
SD (on VHF): I see their name on barges all over the place.
Red (on VHF): They mix the raw materials for cement there: alumina, silica, lime, iron oxide and magnesium oxide together, heat them to 1000 degrees in a kiln and then pulverized the mix to fine powder. Then it's loaded into the barges. They are upgrading the plant to utilize a dry process.
SD (on VHF): A tour of that plant should be interesting.
Red (on VHF): The mixture is dehydrated cement.

SD (on VHF): How is it you come to know so much about cement?
Red (on VHF): I'm a landscape contractor and my business has expanded to the point where I'm using a lot of cement.
SD (on VHF): Landscape, you must be in demand.
Red (On VHF): I'm busy. In fact, I don't even advertise. Word of mouth gets me all my business.
SD (on VHF): Nice position to be in.
SD: Kara, how's Skip's stroke count?
Kara: He's down from a high of 58 to 54.
(Later)
Kara: We're coming up on 2 hours.
SD (looking at the GPS): We're going to pull him. The current has dropped down.
Kara (blowing the signal horn): That's it, Skip.
SD (on VHF): Magic Moment, please pick up Skip.

Scene 2 The Brass Anchor

After the swim we return to the Brass Anchor restaurant. The slips were very, very narrow and after the PM swim it was low tide. The props stir up the mud from the bottom when backing into the slip next to Red Grenier's boat, Sunset.
Tied up at Brass Anchor marina after the swim:
Ed (holding a beer in his hand): Do they have a shower here?
Sally: Yes, they do but it's not a very good one.
Ed: I'm going up to take a shower.
Sally: Let me know how you make out.
Sally (to Tim): Tim, you should take a shower.
SD (wondering if Sally is saying something about body odor): Oh, I think I'll wait til Ed gets back.
SD: We need to consolidate some of our gear.
Sally: I love cleaning out junk, pass it over to me and I'll go thru it on shore.
Sally starts laying out gear on the dock and sorting thru it.
Kara: It sure is sunny and hot here.
SD brings over the nets from Sunset: CP (putting his beer down and grabbing the net): What is this?
Ed: It looks like a big flyswatter.
SD: This is the net we use to scoop debris out of Skip's way.
CP: I'm not having *that* on my boat.

SD: Skip needs it.
CP (taking the net from Tim and putting it back on Sunset): It's not going on this boat! You've got to move some of this gear off the boat.
SD: We're doing that.
SD and Sara work on cleaning up excess gear, repacking and rearranging equipment. CP is trying to put his beer into a personalized cozy when it falls overboard between the two boats.
CP: Damn, I can't reach it.
SD: Wouldn't need a net to retrieve it, now would you?
CP (staring at SD in shock then with resolve): No.
SD (glancing over the side): It's sinking.
CP: This is making me mad.
SD: Sometimes, God talks to us through irony.
CP (giving up and taking a swig): Maybe he'll talk to me through this beer.
Ed returns from the shower.
Ed: That shower was terrible. I could barely get enough water to come out of the shower head.
Sally: It made me feel skuzzy.
Ed: You almost need a shower to clean up from the shower.
SD: I think I'll wait until the next marina to take a shower.
Sally: Oh, no, Tim, you should take a shower.
SD: I'm going to take a pass on this shower.
Tim moves over to Sunset and talks to Skip.
SD: It's eleven o'clock; I'm going up to the restaurant for lunch and get out of this hot sun. Anybody want to come?
Skip: Andy and I might come up later. Could you take some thing up to Andy's car that we don't need.
SD: Sure.
SS: Tim could you make some of the calls.
SD: Who'd you have in mind?
SS: We need to contact the press that saw us off in Albany. I've been trying to keep them advised. Now that we're approaching Rockland County, we need to alert the newspapers there. Plus we need to line up the volunteers for the next week.
SD: Give me the list; I'll see what I can do.
At the restaurant, Tim asks for a table off to the side when he can work on his computer and make phone calls. Andy and Sally

joined him later. On the way out he notices Kara and Ed eating at a table together.
(Later after lunch, scene changes to gas dock)
Sally: Tim, there is a boat at the gas dock asking for you.
SD: Okay.
SD goes down to the gas dock along the riverfront. Finds Runabout II but no one was on board. He put another fender along the side of the boat due to the wave action. The owner returns.
SD: Is this your boat?
Jim: Yes, are you Tim?
SD: Yes, I am.
Jim: I'm Jim Irving; I'm here to help out with the swim.
SD: Great, I have just the job for you.
Jim: Whatever it is, we'll need to get gas.
SD: Let me get Skip's credit card.
SD tracks down Skip aboard Fred's boat, Sunset.
SD: Skip, Jim Irving has showed up.
Skip: Oh, great. I think he's just after a tank of gas.
SD: Well, he's here. I plan on using him to test the current ahead of time. I'll go down to the start and anchor up and check the current then call you when you have to be there.
SS: All right. Here's my card. I think they are just taking advantage of me.
SD fills up the boat and then they cast off to go downriver. As Tim checks Magic Moment for his personal gear, he notices Ed and Kara napping together up on the flying bridge; Kara has made a pillow out of Ed's feet.

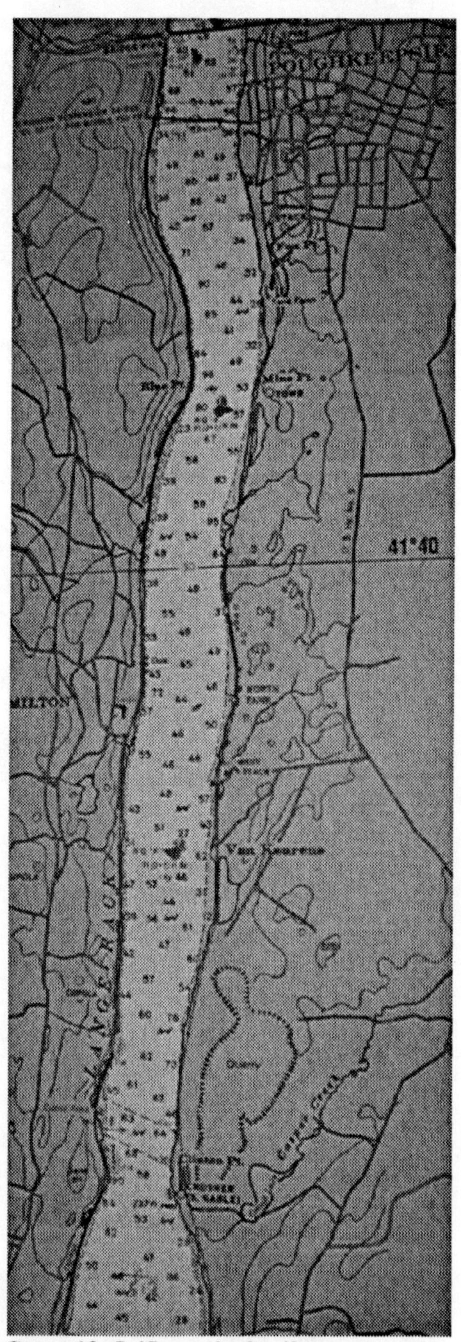

Stage 12 5.45 nautical miles.

Stage 13

Scene 1 Mooning incident

Sunday, August 21st, PM swim. Start time 6:13 pm. Weather: fairly calm, light airs. Sunset occurs at end of the swim. The team leaves Brass Anchor Restaurant and Marina in Poughkeepsie and travels to Front Street Marina at Newburgh Waterfront after the end of the swim. Scene opens with SD aboard Jim Irving's boat, Runabout II. They were anchored up testing the current just north of Wappingers Falls south of the cement plant.

Jim: This is some beautiful day.

SD: It certainly is.

Jim: Would you mind if I go in swimming.

SD: Okay with me. Do you have a safety line to drop behind the boat?

Jim: I'll make one up.

SD: I have to test the current. Got any pretzels?

Jim: Look in the kitchen on the left.

SD (to Jim): I couldn't find any pretzels but these goldfish crackers should work.

Jim jumps in and floats around holding onto the safety line the whole time.

SD (taking a break from his water testing): Hey, Jim, the chart says this section of the river is a no discharge zone. What's the story?

Jim: Oh, the water intake for New York City is just downstream by Chelsea.

SD: New York City drinks Hudson River water?

Jim: I think it's a backup source and it's filtered.

SD: So Skip is swimming in New York City's drinking water; imagine that.

(Later)

SD (to VHF): Magic Moment, Magic Moment this is Runabout II.

CP (on VHF): This is Magic Moment, go ahead Runabout.

SD: We'll need Skip down here around 6 pm. Current is picking up right now.

CP: When do you want us to cast off?

SD: It'll take you about twenty minutes to get down here so leave at 5:40 pm.

CP: We're on our way.
(Later)
Ed (on VHF): Runabout, this is Magic Moment.
SD (on VHF): Go ahead Magic Moment.
Ed (on VHF): We're overheating on our starboard engine. We're going to stop and investigate. What do you want to do about the swimmer?
SD: (a slight pause, on VHF) All right, put Skip on Fred's boat to transport him down here so we can get the swim started on time.

Skip shows up and is started by Sally off Sunset. Sally takes up a position on Fred bow to watch the swim. Jim pull anchor and we join Red downstream. In the distance, Magic Moment is seen approaching. When Magic Moment joins the group, Brian Pickering drops his pants and moons Sally. I break up laughing but am disturbed that something has gone on between them. Kara is aboard Magic Moment.

SD (on VHF): Now that everyone's together, if Magic Moment could launch the dinghy, Brian will motor it over to me and I can take him back to his boat then I'll go pick up Sally.
Sally (on VHF): That's not going to work; Skip just wanted to swim off Red's boat.
SD (on VHF impatiently): What? (pausing) I'm still the Swim Director. I'll decide how the swim is run.
SD (on VHF to Magic Moment): Magic Moment, could you launch the dinghy.
Ed (on VHF): Right on it.
SD (frustrated to Jim): It happens on every swim; someone usurps authority and starts changing things.

Scene 2 Separate swims

SD eventually gets the dinghy and motors around without picking up Sally. She sits on the bow of Sunset staring at Skip. SD pulls in for some close-up pace readings.
SD (on VHF): It looks like Skip went in at the current peak and now the current is dropping.
(Later, while going by Storm King Mountain)

SD (to no one): So this is Storm King (stares at the mountain, glances at the GPS) Great speed.
Sally (on VHF): We're getting close to the two-hour mark.
SD (pulls over by Sally): Hold up blowing the horn; we're practically at the bridge. He's seen it and would, I'm sure, like to make the swim end at the bridge. It's a good goal.
Sally: Okay. (Yelling to Skip) Go for it.
Skip makes the bridge. Sally blows the horn twice. Skip stops stroking.
SD: Skip, good swim; six miles, baby!
SD (on VHF): Magic Moment, please pick up Skip.
SD motors over to Sunset.
SD: Sally, should I take you over to Magic Moment so you can work on Skip?
Sally: You'll have to; my gear is over there.

Scene 3 Front Street marina

Scene opens on the flying bridge of Magic Moment finds Ed, CP, Kara, and Tim together.
Ed (drink in hand): This is Front Street Marina at Newburgh. You find several happening spots: The Blue Martini, Café Pitti, Cena 2000, the River Grill, Torches on the Hudson, Big Easy Bistro, and Havana.
CP (putting down his beer): Don't forget Gully's Restaurant. At this time of night, we'll be lucky to find anything open.
Ed: We'll start at one end of the street and check them out.
Kara: I'm going with you.

Scene 4 Team management problems

After tying up at Front Street Marina, Tim bumps into Jim Irving limping down the dock.
SD: Jim, you don't look so good.
Jim: My back went out.
SD: You know, we have some expert help for that sort of thing, come on aboard and I'll introduce you to Sally.
Tim and Jim Irving go aboard Magic Moment. Brian and Ed are sitting about the stern drinking.
SD: Sally, this is Jim Irving, he's the owner of Runabout II.
Sally: Hi.

SD: His back is hurting and I was wondering if you'd be able to help him out. You know how much we need another boat.
Sally (her eyes light up): You're right! Jim let's go down to your boat and see what I can do for you.
Sally goes off with Jim.
(Tim closes the salon door after Sally leaves)
SD (to Skip): Brian mooned Sally.
SS (surprised): What?
SD: He mooned her.
SS: She didn't say anything.
SD: I don't know what went on but it's intolerable. I have to fire him.
SS: Without the boat, the swim is over.
SD: I know.
SS: These guys have been acting like imbeciles.
SD: Look, I can suck it up and figure something out.
SS: Okay but we can't lose the boat without a replacement.
(Later, Sally returns alone)
Sally: Jim back is in bad shape. He may not be able to join us for the next stage. He's sleeping on shore tonight and will show up in the morning if he's able. He left the boat open so you can sleep on it, Tim.
SS: That guy is just along for the tank of gas.

Scene 5 Swimmer shoulder problems
(Scene shift to Runabout II)
That night, about midnight, Skip calls Tim on his cell phone. Tim was dozing on Runabout II and he fumbles in the dark to find his cell phone.
SD (on his cell phone): Hello.
SS (on his cell phone): Tim, my shoulder's blown up. Can you get Sally to come over?
SD (on his cell phone): Which boat are you on?
SS (on his cell phone): My friend's boat across the dock from the really large ship.
SD: I'm on my way.
SD (walking along the dock, thinking): The swim is over. I wonder if I can get a bus out of Newburgh for New York.
SD goes aboard Sunset and knocks on the hatch. Red answers and Tim goes below to wake Sally.

SD: Sally, Skip needs you. He said his shoulder has blown up.
Sally: I'll be right there.
SD accompanies Sally down to Skip's location. Sally goes in.
Tim hangs around waiting topside. After about 5 minutes, Andy, Skip's wife, pops her head up.
Andy: Tim, can you come inside.
Tim goes below to see Skip in bed surround by his wife and Sally.
Sally: Is there any water around? Skip is just dehydrated. We've check the muscle and everything is okay.
SD: We're out of water. I can check on Jim's boat.
SS (weakly): I sat out in the sun all afternoon.
Sally: He's going to need water.
SD: I could make a run to an all-night deli.
Andy: Okay, take my car.
SD: I'll get some ice.
Tim makes a water run and is back around 2am. Back in the boat with Skip he pours two glasses of water filled with ice cubes. He hands one to Skip lying in bed. Lifts the glasses
SD: Skip, here's to you.
SS: Thanks, Tim.

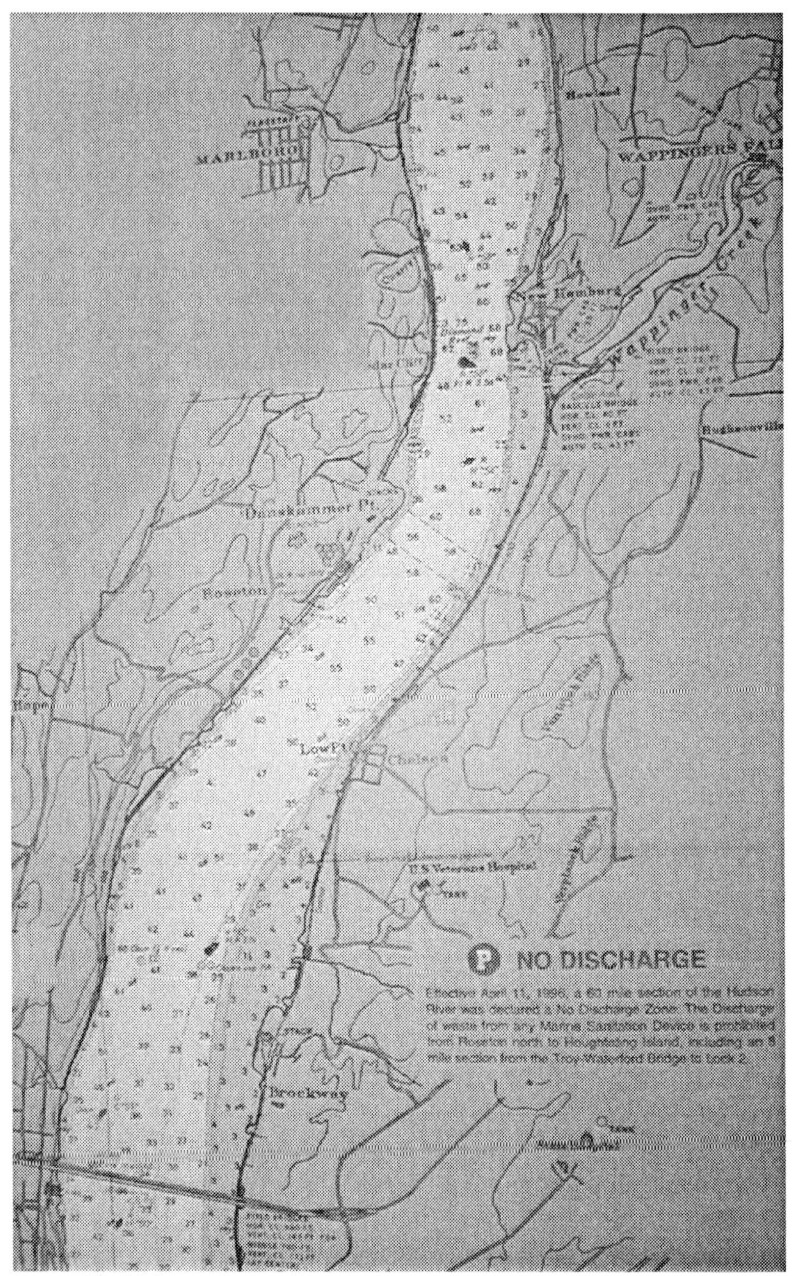

Stage 13 6.23 nautical miles.

Stage 14

Scene 1 Team leadership

Monday, August 22nd, AM swim with a 6:45 am start. Weather: clear light airs, wind switched around from south to north. Starting location: just south of the Newburgh-Beacon Bridge. Scene opens on the stern of Magic Moments tied up at Front Street Marina before the swim.

SD (to Brian who just woke up): Brian, I have to talk with you about yesterday.

CP: Humph. (Listening)

SD: Did you moon Sally?

CP: Why, yes.

Ed (from the flying bridge): Yeah, it was pretty funny.

SD: I know, I was laughing up a storm. It was hilarious. The problem is we're a team. We have to work together. We have to respect each other.

Ed (in explanation): She dropped the radiator cap overboard.

SD (ignoring Ed and speaking to CP): If a gentleman can moon a lady he can apologize to her. I'd like you to apologize to Sally.

CP: (numb silence).

SD walks off.

Ed: What was that about?

CP: I don't know but I'm not doing any apologizing.

(Later, while walking down the dock at the marina before the swim)

SD: Sally, you've been doing a great job on the swim. You're a valuable member of the team. It wouldn't happen without you. I'm glad you're here.

Sally: Thank you.

SD: I asked Brian to apologize to you for mooning you.

Sally: That'll be the day.

SD: Well, if it happens, just accept his apology.

Sally: We'll see if he does.

SD: He may not, I can't force him to but I asked him to.

Scene 2 Pre-swim planning

The only support boat is Magic Moment. Everyone is aboard. Crew keeps to themselves and swim team doesn't talk much.

SD: We've got a nice big stretch of the river to cover today.

SS: This is the last straightaway before the Hudson takes some turns. I'd like to swing in close to the western shore.
SD: The Hudson looks like it narrows a bit near Cornwall. We should get a bump out of that.
SS: What's Cornwall?
SD: It looks like it's a small village down at the base of Storm King Mountain. The mariners guide to the Hudson says there are docks at Cornwall.
SS: I remember that David Scholer up in Albany offered to let us use the docks at Cold Spring Harbor. He's the vice-Commodore of the club.
SD: All right, I'll see if we can get dockage there. Start time is 6:30am. I'll gather everybody up.
SD (to Red): Are you coming along today?
Red: Yes, but after the swim I'll take off and bring my boat down to Haverstraw Marina. You'll be there soon enough.
Bumping into Sally on the way off the boat.
SD: Sally, are you and Skip coming down to Magic Moment?
Sally: We'll be there.
SD back on Magic Moment waits for Skip and Sally to arrive from Sunset. After they come aboard...
SD: Okay, let's cast off.

Scene 3 Another six mile swim
Scene opens after dropping Skip in the water, Sally and Tim are aboard the dinghy.
SD: Sally, this swim looks pretty easy. It's a nice wide channel.
Sally: Okay.
Sally: (blowing the whistle): What's the distance?
SD: Point two seven nautical miles. Not bad for five minutes of swimming.
SD: Sally, we're heading for the white specks at the base of the mountain ahead of us.
Sally: Is that a town?
SD: It's supposed to be Cornwall and they have a yacht club there. We'll come fairly close to shore.
(Later)
Sally (blowing signal horn): Is that the distance? (Looking at the GPS).

SD: Yes, the display shows the distance from the start and the speed.
Sally: One point four two for the 1st half hour.
SD: That's a good indication this swim will be all right.
Sally: What are we looking for?
SD: We need five miles minimum out of each swim. When we hit six, we're golden.
(Later)
CP (on VHF): We have a southbound tug.
SD (picks up GPS and starts to talk. He realizes the 3 items on the seat in front of him {tape machine, VHF, and GPS} have been misplaced: replaces the GPS with the VHF, motions like he is playing 3-card Monty and shrugs, the boys on the bridge of Magic Moment just stare): We can stay on the red buoy side.
Ed (on VHF): We'll relay the information.
(Later)
Sally: So what other games do you play, Tim?
SD: Well, did I tell you about the time Jane Katz and I pretended to be married?
Sally: Who's Jane Katz?
SD: Jane was Skip's swim stroke coach at one time and she has a number of books out on water aerobics.
Sally: Why'd you pretend to be married?
SD: Jane and I were on Skip's environmental swim down Long Island Sound. It wasn't going too well and at Stanford where we pulled in, things were getting ugly.
Sally: Ugly?
SD: The crew whom were volunteers was angry. At the team meal, you could cut the tension with a knife. We were staying at the downtown Sheraton and that night they were having a high school reunion: Staples High School, class of 1984. So I announced that I was going dancing after the meal and Jane pipes up that she would go with me.
Sally: Where did you go dancing?
SD: At the reunion.
Sally: You didn't go there, how'd you get in?
SD: Crashed it with a little help from the press.
Sally: How'd the press help you get into the reunion, did you pretend you were covering the reunion for the paper.

SD: No, we'd of had to show ID but that's not a bad idea for next time. Our picture was on the front page of the Stanford Advocate and when we explained we were on a swim, I pointed to our picture on the paper they were reading and they waved us right in like we were celebrities.
Sally: No kidding.
SD: The married part was our cover so when we sat down we'd have something to talk about with the attendees. It was hilarious. I told Jane we had five children and she was upset she had that many kids.
Sally: I bet she was.
SD: So while we were dancing the night away, I noticed one woman staring at me. As we are dancing, Jane says to me that one member of the class was a porn star.
Sally: What?
SD: That was exactly what I said. First of all, I've no idea where Jane got this information but the next thing you know, we're looking at all the women trying to figure out who it is.
Sally: Who was it?
SD: Sally, you're rushing me…about half an hour later we're taking a break and this woman that was staring at me comes rushing over to us. That was Marilyn Briggs, aka Marilyn Chambers.
Sally: Really.
SD: Yes, the way I figure it, she was eyeing me because I was the only male in the school she hadn't "dated" and she wanted to figure out whom it was that got away.
Sally: Oh, now you're being modest.
SD: It turns out Marilyn wasn't the best-looking girl in the class. I saw at least ten better-looking women. But I did get her signature.
Sally: I have to do some work here.
Sally (blowing the signal horn): Hour and one half.
SD: Write the distance down as four point three four but it's actually greater since we've turned left at Cornwall.
Sally: How's that.
SD: The GPS reads direct distances from here to the start; we've turned a corner so the distance isn't reading correctly. Besides, our speed is up to over 3 knots. I'm reading three ones and three twos.

(Later)
SD: Have you noticed all the railroad trains headed north?
Sally: Yes.
SD: At Front Street Marina I heard them all night long. There sure is a lot of commerce moving around by trains and barges in this river valley.
Sally: I haven't given it much thought.
SD: Just something I noticed sitting out here. At one time, the Erie Canal was the lifeblood of the nation. The Hudson River was the conduit between the canal and New York City. Looks like its still serving the nation.
(Later)
Sally: We're coming up on two hours.
SD: Let's call the swim here; we're right off the yacht club at Cold Spring. How convenient.
Sally (blowing the signal horn twice): That's it, Skip.
SD: Looks like another six miles.
SS: Great.

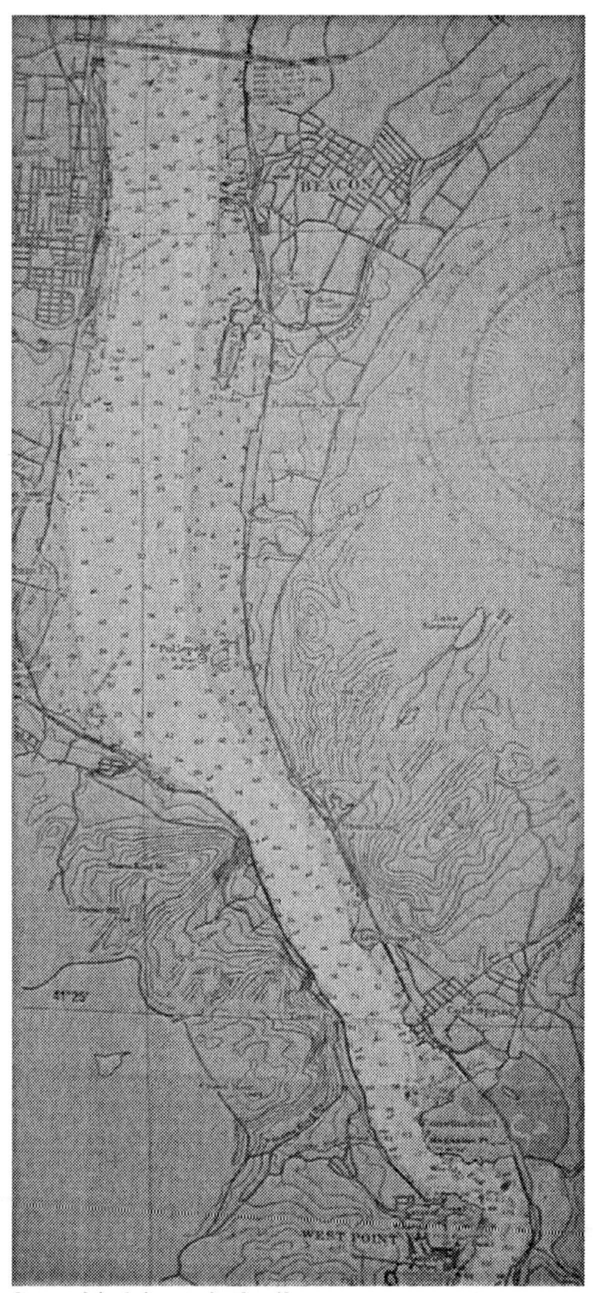

Stage 14 6.4 nautical miles.

Stage 15

Scene 1 Cold Spring Boat Club

Monday, August 22nd, PM swim with a 7:12 pm starting time. Weather is clear and hot. Scene opens aboard the flying bridge of Magic Moment as they arrive at Cold Spring Boat Club after the finish of stage 14 in the morning.
SD: Brian, that's Cold Spring Boat Club. We can tie up there until tonight.
CP: Why don't we go back to Front Street Marina?
SD: Well, at Front Street we have to pay for the dockage and here it's free.
CP: I don't like tying up along the outside docks. Every wake rocks the boat.
SD: Let's go and see what it is like.
CP: Okay, but I'd rather go to Front Street. Look at the way that dock is pitching.
SD: I'll help you put some fenders out.

CP and Tim check in with the Boat Club, signing their guest log. They make a trip uptown for ice with a ride courtesy of a member. After they return, Tim sets up office under the club canopy looking out over the marina. Sally is seen sitting out under a tree on a bench the town has set up talking on the cell. Later she is seen sitting on a picnic table with laundry in the shade of a tree at the yacht club and CP wanders over, talks to her then falls asleep on his laundry. Sally wanders off.

Scene 2 Lunch

Skip and SD are walking up the boat ramp to go to lunch when they encounter Sally.
SD: Sally, want to go up town for lunch?
Sally: I've all ready been. It's really nice. There's an ice cream store off the main street by the railroad tracks. There is an outfitters store up there, too.
SD: Hmmm, maybe I'll check out buying another pair of cargo pants.
Tim and Skip go uptown walking under the railroad tracks. They stop outside Cathryn's Tuscan Grill.
SD: Skip, we could keep walking but this place looks like it has air conditioning.

SS: Fine with me.
The entrance is set back near the rear of the building and the yard is decorated with eclectic yard art.
SD: This is a real artsy town.
SS: The town is seeing a revival.
SD: I like it. Here's the entrance.
Tim and Skip enjoy an Italian lunch and spend about two hours resting. They discuss the formation of a swimming committee to sanction swims down the Hudson.
SD: Skip, what do you think about when you are swimming?
SS: Oh, the first five minutes I'm thinking about everything: here we go again, why I'm in the water, rationale and then eventually I begin to get into the swim.
SD: How's that?
SS: I've memorized every inch of the swim so when I let go of what I can't do anything about, I take control of my swim. It's all about focusing on the swim: keeping my balance so the swim goes well and worry about the old injuries and keeping them at bay.
SD: Well, you're to be congratulated because if you fall apart, the swim is over.
SS: I'm really dialed into the swim. Sometimes I just increase my stroke count but not pull as hard, pulling shallower as well as not as deep and gliding. I try to be as efficient as possible. I look to utilize the roll and take torque off the shoulders and make myself more streamlined.
SD: What do you think about the Hudson for swimming?
SS: I'm thinking of organizing a swim committee to sanction swims on the Hudson.
SD: Skip, I'm seeing all kinds of great swims down the Hudson: short swims of two hours duration and longer ones between two bridges.
SS: I'd like to come back next year and arranging a relay swim.
SD (thinking): Wow, if you had more than one team, they could compete against each other.
SS: Yes, and I'd organize it.
SD: With teams being what they are, you'll have one team out in front and others bring up the rear. I have an idea. After the first race, have the teams vote a team member off the team and each team gets one of the other team members. Basically, the slow

team gets a swimmer from the fast team. By the end of the race, all the teams should be of equal ability and the last swim will be very tight.
SS: Interesting.
SD: Plus, some swimmers may not be able to show up for the entire swim so you should allow swimmers to enter for just a section.
SS: What do you mean?
SD: You did Mid Hudson Bridge to Newburgh Beacon Bridge in just two swims. That's four hours. That's an easy swim for trained athletes. Today's swim could have very easily ended at Cornwall.
SS: Okay, let's think up some names for this committee.
SD: Well, Manhattan had MIMS, the Montauk swim I called MOMS. This swim needs to incorporate Hudson somehow in the name…
SS: HUMS for Hudson Marathons Swim, the Hu is from Hudson? (Laughing)
SD: Whatever works. (pause) You know you're ahead of the human record.
SS: What, how do you figure that? We're not finished.
SD: The average speed for Creegan's swim was two point six miles per hour. You're at two point seven at this point in the swim.
SS: How are you getting his average speed?
SD: I take the distance, 150 miles, and divide it by the total time. I figure your average time by the distance you've covered so far divided by the time it's taken.
SS: I'm ahead of the record! What was the dog's average speed?
SD: Two point nine.
SS: Oh, my. That's fast.
SD: Yes, one fast dog. We're creeping up slowly but we've a ways to go.
SS: Think our team is going to pull together?
SD: Well, the heat yesterday at the Brass Anchor was disastrous. You got dehydrated and the Corona boys just hydrated themselves with beer and wound up drunk. I saw Sally and the captain sitting at the same picnic table in the shade of the tree earlier. It looks like they were talking. I told him to apologize to Sally.

SS: Okay, let's pay the bill and head back. I need to rest a bit.
SD: Let me get it. I think the crew money has disappeared.
SS: You're kidding me. I gave Fred $900 for food expenses which he handed over to Brian.
SD: The captains have been spending the money rather liberally and I think there was only $300 left when Magic Moment took over.
SS: Well, I think I can get another credit card and come up with some more money. If I have to, I'll do it. I don't want money to be a reason the swim fails.
SD: Skip, I don't mind paying for my meals. You've been more than generous.
SS: Tim, I pulled $10,000 from my saving to hire the boats, the therapists, and you. I've promised everyone I'd cover their expenses. I'm not letting this stand in the way; I want this record.
SD: Okay.
SD (calls out): Oh, waitress, could I have the check?
SS: The air conditioning in this restaurant has been great.
Skip and Tim return to the ship window-shopping through the town. Tim stops at the ice cream parlor for another repast.

Scene 3 Hells Gate

The scene opens with pre-swim planning discussion between SD and Skip aboard Magic Moment.
SS: We're going to be seeing some eddies off West Point.
SD: Well, I'll try and steer you around the eddies as best I can.
SS: It's going to be wild. (Pulling the map out) Let's go over the course.
SD: This is probably going to be a little bit like Hell's Gate.
SS: That was a spooky swim.
SD: You were the second swimmer I took through Hell's Gate.
SS: Who was the other?
SD: Chris Green, the English swimmer.
SS: I remember on that swim the water pulling at me.
SD: Well, if we could do Hell's Gate, I'm confident we'll do all right here. Skip, I think you are the only person to have swum the entire length of the East River. Do you remember your time?
SS: It was five and one half hours.

SD: Probably shorter because you went all the way to the Statute of Liberty.
SS: Yes and *you* had me swim through the Spider.
SD: Yeah but the current had dropped by the time you got there and I've had other people swim through there.
SS: What do you think happened when the harbor police lost a diver there?
SD: He was in the water playing the victim for a lifesaving exercise. You know when you're doing that exercise in a pool; the victim goes underwater to simulate a more difficult rescue. Only in his case, he was sitting right on the top of the division between the East River and the Hudson. There's a shear wall separating the hydraulic forces; the Hudson was running south and the East River west. When they butt up against each other, they don't merge. The East River turns down to mix along the bottom. He was sitting on the top of a waterfall. It's so sad, he was doomed; but who knew?
SS: It was a terrible loss.
SD: This isn't psyching you up for your swim.
SS: Tim, remember I've swum through here before. After we get around West Point I want to hit the shore over by Garrison then move back across the river to get the current along the bend by Bear Mountain Bridge.
SD: Gotcha.

Scene 4 The End of the World
Scene opens with SD and Sally aboard the dinghy right off the docks of Cold Spring Boat Club.
SD (to Sally): Nice to see the yacht club members came down to see us off.
SD: Let's get this started. Skip's in the water.
Sally: Ready, Go. (Blows signal horn)
SD: You know, it deceptive the way the river runs up ahead.
Sally: That's why they call it Worlds End.
In the first five minutes they make the bend and are looking at the campus of West Point Military Academy. The eddy pools lie ahead.
SD: I'm like to bring Skip out away from the shoreline, let's have him go left.
Sally: Okay.

SD (staring ahead reading the water): Have him go left again.
Sally: There's a lot of turbulence here and up ahead.
SD: This is Worlds End. We'll be making a lot of course changes here.
SD (to Sally): Go left.
SD (to Sally): Go right.
SD (to Sally): Go right.
SD (to Sally): Go left again.
SD (to Sally): We're getting too close to the shore. Have him go left again.
SD (to Sally): divert right.
SD (to Sally): divert left.
SD (to Sally): now we have to have him swim hard to the left for a while.
Sally: That's the last of the eddies.
SD: Looks like it.
SD (eyeing the range down to Bear Mt. Bridge): Okay, we're past Gees Point, have him turn right.
SD (to Sally): He wants to swing close to the eastern shore at some point. But I think the current will take him there.
Sally: He's getting difficult to see.
SD: I seem to drifting away from him too easily or he's swimming away from the boat deliberately. I wonder if he smells the engine fumes.
(Later)
Magic Moment is seen coming into view. Captain Pickering is on the bow singing. He's wearing his brown short, boat shoes and a pink hat. A Corona beer is seen in his hand.
SD: My God, I'm going to have to make the play a musical.
(Later)
SD: I wish Skip wasn't dead set on swimming to the western shore under Bear Mountain Bridge. He only needs to turn and go with the current flowing south. Maybe he's feeling the current running.
Sally: Do you want me to tell him to turn left again?
SD: No, he's seen our last indication and didn't change course. No point in arguing with him, we'll just lose the argument and upset him.
Sally: It's really getting dark.
SD: We're going to have to put a light stick on him.

Sally: What is that?
SD: It's like those glow necklaces kids get at a circus only it has a place to attach it with a safety pin to clothing.
Sally: Oh, I know what you mean.
SD: Fishermen attach them to their clothing when they are working offshore, in case they fall in.
Sally: Two hours is coming up.
SD: This is going to coincide with his passing right under the bridge. How convenient. Isn't this the Bear Mountain Bridge?
Sally: Yes.
Sally (blowing the signal horn twice, it breaks apart): That's screwy. Distance?
SD (signaling to Skip): Six point six seven nautical miles. What a swim!
SS: Tim, I could feel the current pushing on me going through World's End but Hell's Gate was worse.

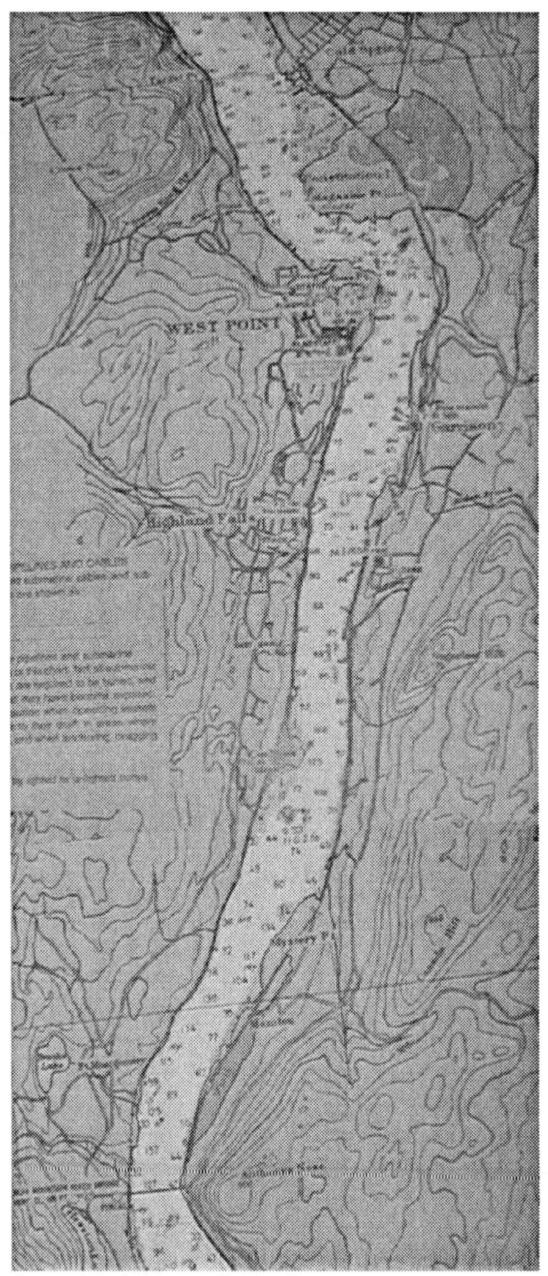

Stage 15 6.67 nautical miles.

Stage 16

Scene 1 Haverstraw Bay

Tuesday, August 23rd, AM swim with a 7:07 start time. Weather: windy out of the north. Swim team is now located at Haverstraw Marina, the largest marina on the East Coast after this stage having arrived there the night before from the Bear Mountain Bridge. Scene opens up aboard the bridge of Magic Moment on the ride back up to Bear Mt. Bridge for the start just as the Magic Moment is passing under the overhead power cables strung across the Bay south of Peekskill and the nuclear power plant. Kara has rejoined the swim.

SD (to Kara): You know, if Skip makes it this far, to these power lines, he'd have a good swim this morning.

SD: Brian, can you swing over by the buoy by the nuclear plant. I need to take a look at the current on that side of the river.

CP: What ever you say.

SD: Looking good. Let's take another look at the green buoy on the other side.

CP (pointing off to the left at a buoy): Over there?

SD: Yes, and slow down just a bit.

SD (peering over the side): Looking good. It looks like the current is better on the green side away from the power plant. Let's head for the bridge. I'm going down to talk to Skip.

(On the stern of Magic Moment)

SS: Tim, I don't want to be over by the power plant. Last time I was down here I came out of the water beet red, the water was so hot over there.

SD: Skip, don't worry, it looks like the green side is faster. We just have to hold you over on that side.

SS (looks behind the boat as we head north): Should I head up on the smoke stack?

SD: Which one?

SS (pointing): The white one.

SD: Looks good.

SS: As long as we got our signals straight. I just don't want to be over by the power plant.

SD: Skip, you won't be. (Looking at the computer) Your average is two point eight. You're creeping up on the dog's record.

SD (to Ed): We're just about there, pull up right under the bridge, by the time we launch; we'll have drifted right onto the location.
Sally: I'll get him ready.
SD: Who's with me in the dinghy?
Sally: Kara.
SD: Gotcha.
Sally and Kara go to work on Skip in the salon of Magic Moment, singing song with made up lyrics and telling dirty jokes. Skip enjoyed this session quite a bit.

Scene 2 Swimming with nukes
Aboard the dinghy we find SD and Kara.
Kara: When should we start him?
SD: As soon as possible, we're drifting too fast.
Kara: Skip, Ready, Go.
SD: We drifted about 100 yards south of the start. Darn!
Kara: 5 minutes (blows whistle) Distance?
SD: Point three nine. Boy, we're moving. We'll have to see if this holds.
Kara: 10 minutes (blows whistle).
SD: Point six four. I thought so, looks like the speed was influence by the abbreviated start. We'll have to make up this distance on his next start.
Kara: Could you see if there is a Mountain Dew in the container?
SD: Yes, I packed one. (Handing it to her)
Kara: and the goldfish crackers?
SD: Right here.
Kara: I just love this breakfast food.
SD: How is it you are here today?
Kara: I've got the day off. The rest of the week I can make the morning swims as I work in the afternoon.
SD: Did I mention I was going to write a play about the swim?
Kara: No. How could you write a play? What would be in it?
SD: Well, it'd be about everything that goes on. I talk to people all the time and they are very curious about what we're doing.
Kara: Doesn't sound like it'll be very interesting.
SD: It'd be about two people in a rubber dinghy. You wouldn't even see the swimmer.
Kara: That's what I mean.

SD: It's really about the river.
Kara (Suddenly enlightened): Oh.
SD: Plus, it depends on how well I can write it.
Kara: You'd have to put in what the swimmer says like, "Which way?"
SD (laughing): That's for sure.
SD (fussing with the audio tape machine): My tape machine isn't working. Kara, could you write down some notes?
Kara: Okay.
SD: Kara, we're looking at keeping Skip on the green side of the channel today.
Kara: Okay.
SD: We're not doing too badly, so far. Skip didn't want to get near the nuclear power plant south of Peekskill.
(Later)
Kara: Tim, here are the power lines. You said on the way up that if we make the power lines, Skip would be doing great.
SD: That's right. This is great. What's the time?
Kara: Hour twenty.
SD: He's picked up some decent current! I was worried he'd be carried over by the nuclear plant but it didn't happen.
(Later)
SD: Kara, we need to have Skip take a wide turn here. I'd like to keep him out of the dead water south of the power plant at Tompkins Cove.
Kara: Is that a nuclear plant?
SD: No, you can tell a nuclear plant by the dome over one building.
(Bit later)
SD: Kara, signal him to come to the boat. We're too close to shore.
Kara: Look at that broken down ship over there. It looks like a pirate ship.
SD: Yes, it does.
Kara: Your play should be called Pirates of the Hudson. Do you think we can get Johnny Depp to star in it? I want to star in it, too.
SD: I don't see why not.
Kara: Sally said you did some play-acting.
SD: Want me to set a scene?

Kara: Sure.
SD (into Bogie character by end of sentence): Well, it'd have to be something where a river is involved. You know, part and parcel of the story. (thinking…) All right, I'm Humphrey Bogart and you're Katherine Hepburn and *this* is the African Queen.
Kate (Kara jumping right in): And what is that? (Pointing at Skip)
Bogie: Why, Miss Rose, that's a crocodile.
Kate: It doesn't look like a crocodile.
Bogie: See, that's the beauty of it. It's a disguise.
Kate: Looks like a human to me!
Bogie: Aw, and that's where you're wrong. Why no sooner you'd hand that swimming crocodile a drink and it'd rise up and bite your arm off.
Kate: Mr. Allnut, you can't fool me. You might think I'm a frustrated, fidgety old maid but I can tell a man from a crocodile. Some men might be crocodiles but after you civilize them I think you'll find they are quite docile.
Bogart: They're just biding their time, Miss, just biding their time.
Kate: Is that what you think, Mr. Allnut.
Bogart: I'm thinking that if you think I'm going to take this boat all the way down to the mouth of this here river, you're crazy!
Kate: Maybe I am, Mr. Allnut. Maybe I am.
SD: Well, I've run out of ideas…
(Later)
SD: Kara, it looks like the engine fumes are drifting onto Skip. I'm going to switch sides.
(Later)
Kara: Coming up on two hours.
SD: My god, we're coming up on Stony Point. Let's line him up on the next green buoy.
SD (on VHF): Magic Moment, Magic Moment, could I have a depth reading here?
CP (on VHF): I'm reading 25 feet here.
SD: Kara, let's have him swim away from the boat. (Kara hand signals Skip)
Kara (blows the signal horn twice): Skip, great swim.

SD: I have to go over the numbers because of the turns the river took but it looks like another six-mile swim.

Scene 3 Tanks for the memories
(Later, after being dropped back at the Haverstraw marina)
Stranger (on cell phone): We'll be at the marina.
SD: Hello, did I overhear you mention you were retired Navy?
Tank: Yes, I was aviation. I work for the airlines right now. My name is Tank Sherman.
SD: I'm Tim Johnson.
Tank: What is it that you folks are doing here?
SD: We're escorting a swimmer from Albany to New York City. We're trying to set a record.
Tank: That sounds so cool. I'd want to do something like that.
SD: Well, we do need some escort boats for press.
Tank: Come on down to my boat and we'll talk about it.
SD spends the next two hours chatting with Tank aboard his boat.
SD: One problem I'm looking at getting a handle on is when Skip swims around a bend in the river.
Tank: What would be the problem?
SD (sketching out the problem on paper): The water runs fastest on the outside of the curve but the inside curve is the shortest distance. The problem is where in the river should I put the swimmer so he gets the best time: with the fastest current, the shortest distance or some combination of the two?
Tank (overlaying the solution on the paper): Hmmm, airlines have a similar problem when the jet stream develops curves and bends. The more of a push from the jet stream, the less fuel the plane uses. The navigation takes that into account and I've noticed that we'll change course slightly to follow the bend but we don't go for the Markimum wind speed.
SD: Interesting. The variables are probably the radius of the curve, the gradient speed, and the swimmer's speed.
Tank: The airlines have had supercomputers work on this problem. It's a dilly. What's the issue with speed?
SD: We're trying to beat a record that was set by a dog.
Tank: A dog?
SD: Yes, somebody got their dog to swim the Hudson in 44 hours back in 1928.

Tank: How'd they do that?
SD: Not sure but we did figure out that the dog only swam in the peak of the tide.
Tank: How are you doing?
SD: We're behind the dog's pace.
Tank: No.
SD: I've calculated the dog's average time to be two point nine knots and right now, after this morning swim, Skip hit two point eight three. It's not over yet. We've got some fast stretches of water coming up.
Tank: Who else is helping?
SD: Well, we have a massage therapist that is a lesbian.
Tank: Oh.
SD: Yes, every guy that gets on the swim thinks they can fix her.
Tank starts chuckling.
SD: The captain and the mate on the escort boat are drinking up a storm. The other day the captain appeared on the bow dressed in shorts with a pink hat singing a rock and roll song.
Tank: Oh, my.
SD: Then two days ago he mooned the lesbian.
Tank: Really, that's hilarious!
SD: I know, I was laughing up a storm but it bodes ill for the teamwork.
Tank: What do you mean?
SD: Unless you respect each other, you're not going to work together very well; I wanted to fire him.
Tank: Obviously you didn't.
SD: Couldn't, the swim would be over. We don't have another support boat.
Tank: What did you do?
SD: I told him to apologize to her.
Tank: Did he?
SD: I don't know. Say, that's Sally over there.
SD (calling to Sally): Sally, come over here.
Sally: What's up?
SD: Sally, I want you to meet someone, his name is Tank.
Tank: Sally, have you been mooned in the last day or two?
Sally (with tears in her eyes): Yes, but I pretended not to notice.
Tank (taking a deep breath): Mooning is a sign of affection and respect.

(Sally's eyes bug out in disbelief)
Tank: Let me tell you about an incident that happened in 1973 or so. I was a Lieutenant JG in Jacksonville. We were all in dress whites at the officer's club as the fleet had just come in. The Admiral was celebrating his anniversary with his wife. Since he was an Admiral, he's rarely home so this was a special occasion. He and his wife came in and the men, about 500, saluted him and gave him a hurrah. The Admiral and his wife went off to be seated in a private table overlooking the St. John River for their dinner. The Exec wasn't satisfied that we had honored him adequately so he ordered the company commanders to line the officers up and marched us around the building to the banks of the St. John River in view of the Admiral. On command, About Face, Drop trouser, 500 men mooned the Admiral. The Admiral and his wife saluted the men and we left.
SD (in wide eyed admiration): My god, a 500-man moon salute!
Sally: Shocking, to say the least.
SD: Tank, did you want to go out on this evenings swim?
Tank: Oh, I've got my wife's parents on board and we're scheduled to go to dinner.
SD: Well, we'll miss having you along.
SD (to Sally): We better get back.

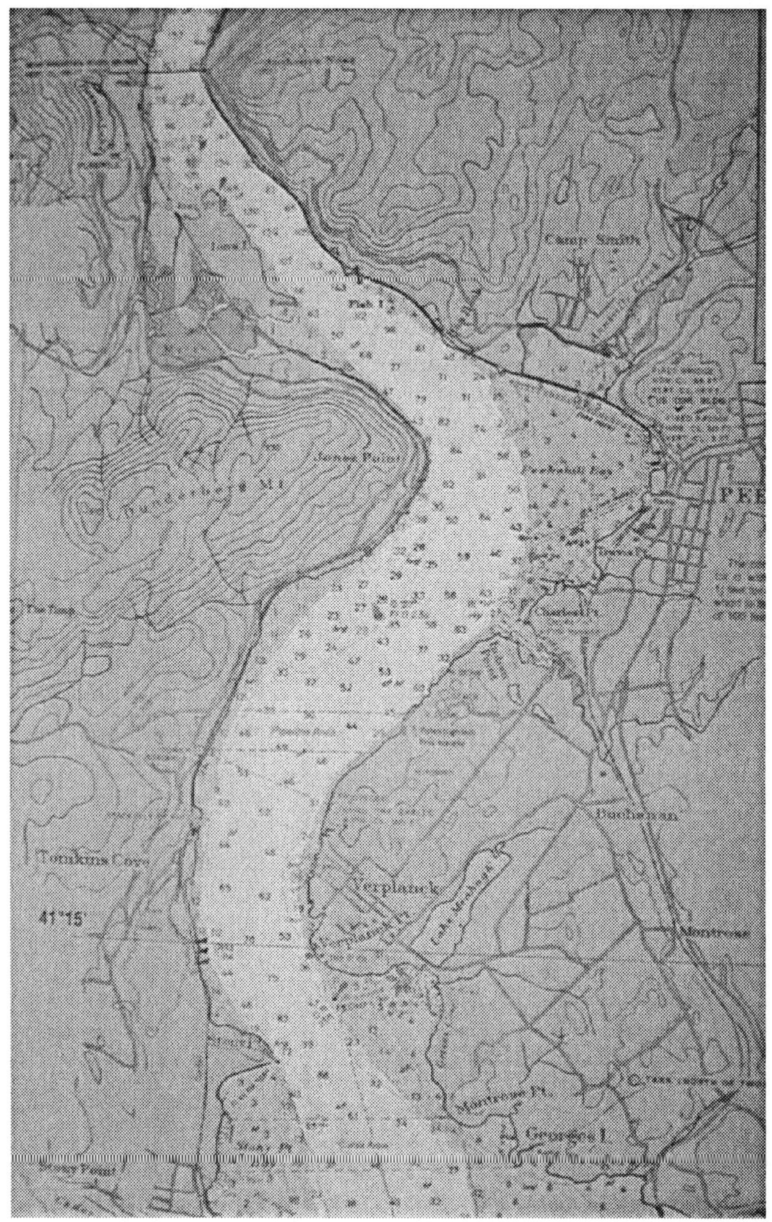

Stage 16 5.92 nautical miles.

Stage 17

Scene 1 New escort boat

Tuesday, August 23rd, PM swim with a 7:03 start time. Weather is calm and clear with light airs out of the east. Location: Haverstraw Marina. Scene opens with SD dockside near Magic Moment on his cell phone talking to a new support boat coming into Haverstraw marina.

SD (on his cell phone): Hello. Bryan, it's good to hear from you. We're at the transit dock. It's at the end of the red pier. I'm wearing a green polo shirt. Can you see that sail boat that motoring in right now? That's right by the red dock. (Bryan's boat pulls into view) You got me.

(Later after tying up)

Bryan: Hi, I'm Bryan Juncosa.

SD: Hello. I'm Tim Johnson, the swim director. Come on down and meet everyone.

SD and Brian walk down the dock to the stern of Magic Moment. SD makes the requisite introductions.

SD: I'm going to ride out with Bryan to the starting location and check the tide flow.

SS: Tim, we can use his boat instead of the dinghy. He has underwater lights.

Tim and Bryan go out on his boat to the starting location off Stonypoint and anchor up.

Tim: Say, do you have anything that we could use as a current marker? I've been using pretzels.

Bryan (from beneath the helm, he pulls out a BJ-sized container of pretzel nuggets): I do have these certified pretzel nuggets.

Tim: Really. My, these will work fine. Let me show you how I've been checking the current.

(Later)

SD: Bryan, we can head back in; this current is right on schedule for a 7 pm start. We'll get the rest of the crew to shake a leg and get this swim started.

SD: My next question to you is can you get this boat to idle below 2 knots.

Bryan: Why?

SD: Skip only makes about 1.7 knots. If you can't slow down enough, you wind up going in and out of gear to stay even with him.

Bryan: I don't know; we'll have to try.
SD: Right here in the marina is as good a spot as any. There's no current.
Bryan: How's this?
SD (reading the GPS): 2.1 knots. We could try a drogue.
Bryan: You have one?
SD: We have the finest Staples file carton that we can drop over the side.
Bryan rigs the drogue.
Bryan: When we drop it, just tend to the lines.
SD: Okay.
Boat gets underway with the drogue in position.
SD: Oh, this is nice, 1.5 knots.
Bryan: Since we'll be running at night, I can rig some halogen lights over the side.
SD: Skip will like that. I'll have to hang them so they don't shine in his eyes.
Boat arrives back at Haverstraw marina. Tim goes over to Magic Moment to get the swim equipment bucket.
SD (to CP): Can we be off the dock by 6:30pm?
CP (putting a beer down): Should be able to do that. Has anyone seen Regional news yet?
SD (to CP): Keep an eye out for them, if they show up, you could always take them out for a shot on the water then bring them back in. But don't wait for them.
SD: Sally, who's on board with me?
Sally: Looks like I am. We need to get a replacement for the signal horn. It didn't work so well the last time I blew it.
SD: I'll look around and put one in the supply bucket.
Brian: Here's one you could use (offering the boat's signal horn).
SD: Okay, thank you. I think Skip had spare bottles on board somewhere. Looks like I'll have to go through the supplies.

Scene 2 Swim or die

At the start aboard Bryan's boat we find Bryan, SD, and Sally.
SD: Okay, this is the starting location just south of Stony Point
SD (in the bow by Sally): Sally, let's get Skip in the water.
Sally (on VHF): Magic Moment, have Skip enter the water.
Sally: Ready for the start?

SD (looking at Skip): Looks like he's ready to go. Let's do it.
Sally (blowing the starting horn): Go for it!
Sally arranges herself on the bow with various items (whistle, horn, watch, cell phone).
SD: What'd you think of Tank?
Sally: He's amazing.
SD: I liked him, too. I wanted to get him out here on the swim but he had commitments for dinner.
Sally: Bummer.
SD (to Bryan): We're going to have to keep Skip to the starboard side of the channel until this northbound tug passes.
SD: Sally, have Skip swim to the right.
Sally (going over the signal in her mind and gesturing): Okay.
Sally: He's not going over.
SD: Keep signaling, we've got to move him. That tug has not slowed down.
SS (stops swimming): What's going on?
SD (to Skip): Tug is coming, Skip.
SS: Not fair!
SD: We can't argue with him.
Skip resumes swimming with an angry splash.
SD (to Bryan, pointing): We're headed straight right down to that mountain. The channel takes us there so we just have to stay with it.
Sally: Tim, stop pointing!
SD: Sally, you've co-op-ed all my gestures.
Sally (chuckling): Guess we have.
Bryan: There is a series of fixed beacons along the shore.
SD: Yes. We can line up on the second one. I'm not worried if he get close to shore there, the current will push him along rather nicely.
Bryan: With Croton Point, it'll be like a jet nozzle.
(Later)
SD: You know when Kara is aboard Magic Moment, it's as if she has mesmerized the "boys."
Sally: That looks like her fetching them beers.
SD (talking to Sally): I think Kara is pretty hung up on Ed.
Sally: You got that one right. I called that two days ago!

SD: I notice the other day that she was using Ed's feet as a pillow when they were trying to sack out on the bridge and at the Brass Restaurant they went to lunch together.
Sally: She follows Ed around like a puppy dog.
SD: Ed's got a great voice. He should be in radio.
Sally: What, in Talk Dirty radio?
SD: You think he talks dirty?
Sally: Those two are gross.
(As it grows darker)
Bryan: Tim, help me rig these lights.
SD: Nice generator! Not noisy at all.
Tim and Bryan rig the light (a halogen lamp in a cage with hooks) over the side of the boat.
SS (while swimming): Fumes!
SD: Bryan, I think that's your boat creating the fumes from the motor. We'll need to switch sides.
Bryan: This is going to be difficult with us towing the drogue.
SD: You could slow down and let him get ahead before moving to the other side.
Bryan: Watch the towline.
SD: Will do, I'll move the lights to the other side.
(Later as they sweep along close to shore off Congers)
SD: We're really moving here.
Bryan: We have the last fixed beacon up ahead we need to clear.
SD (scanning the horizon): What's that structure out there?
Bryan: I think it's a duck blind. It's shallow in there.
(Minutes later)
SD: You know we're really being pushed down into the shallows. This is the start of the underwater shelf along the western shore off Nyack that goes all the way past the Tappan Zee Bridge.
SD (calling up to Sally on the bow): Sally, have Skip swim away from the boat.
Sally (waves the red signal light): Got it.
Bryan: This is going to be close.
SD (moving up to Sally): Sally, signal him to move away from the boat again.
(A bit later)
SD (looking ahead to the fixed beacon): It's almost like he's swimming for his life here.

Sally: The lighthouse is getting closer.
Bryan: I'm moving the boat to the other side of Skip, I don't want to run aground on the light.
SD: I'm tempted to turn him and have him swim on the shallow side of the lighthouse. I just don't know if it's safe.
Skip passes with about 20 feet of clearance
SD: That was some adventure. Let's get him lined up on the red buoys over on the left up ahead.
Bryan: That is Terrytown in the distance.
Sally: Two hours is coming up
SD: Not soon enough for me!
Sally (blowing the signal horn twice): Distance?
SD: Six point one. Nice position to end a swim: at the start of the channel that goes by Tarrytown.
Bryan: I have to work tomorrow but I will be available tomorrow night.
SD: We need you; that would be just fine. Thank you.

After the swim, Sally and Tim ride with Bryan Juncosa downriver to Cornetta's where Bryan ties the boat up. It is not being used for the morning swim, stage 18. Bryan gives the two a ride back to Haverstraw in his vehicle.

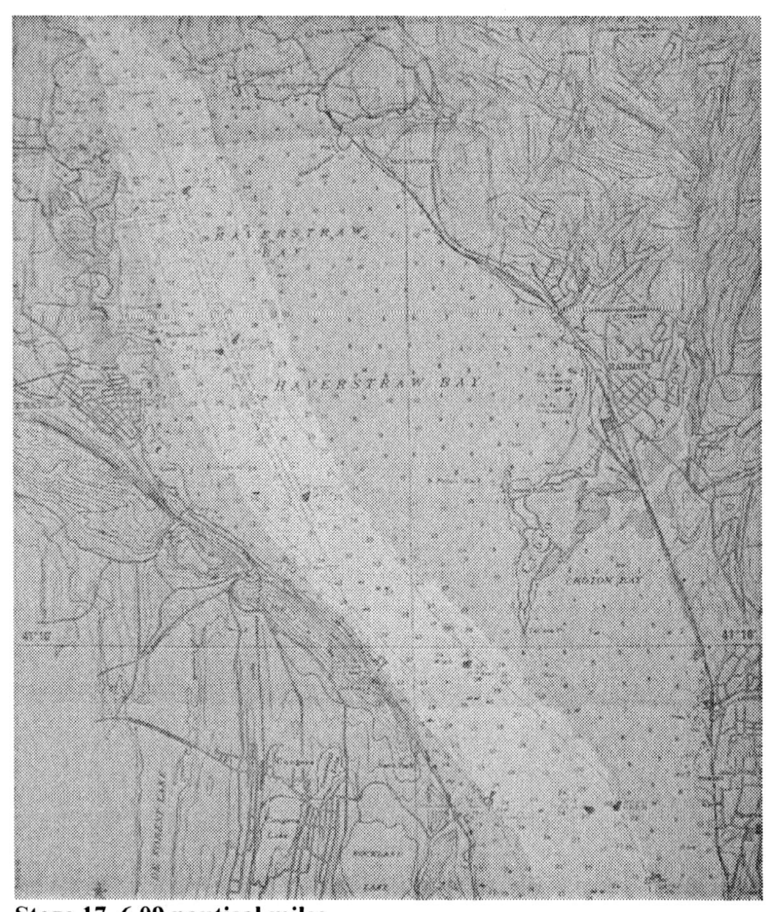

Stage 17 6.09 nautical miles.

Stage 18

Scene 1 Pre-swim planning

Wednesday, August 24th, AM swim with a 7:15 am start. Weather: blows up to 20 knots at the end of the swim with 1-2 foot swells out of the north. The scene opens on the flying bridge of Magic Moment as they run up to the start off Ossining. Ed is at the helm, CP is drinking a beer alongside.

SD (to Ed): Ed, I want to be invited to the wedding.

Ed: What wedding?

SD: Oh, nothing.

Ed (thinking): Better not be a wedding.

SD (to CP): I'd like to take a look at the current. Could you divert the ship so we run by the buoy coming up?

Ship leans left then right.

SD: That's fabulous. Look at that current. It's running straight down the channel.

CP (putting down his beer): What's the expect course tonight.

SD: He should swim from the start to the Tappan Zee Bridge and perhaps beyond. We'll take one of the side channels at the Tappan Zee Bridge so we stay out of the way of commercial traffic.

CP: Okay.

SD (going down to the main deck): Skip, there must be a 30-foot wake coming off that buoy. We'll want to get you in the water ASAP.

SS: There's a shelf along the western side of the Hudson. We'll want to stay in deeper water.

SD: We're moving the start laterally so you're right by the edge of the channel.

SS: I don't want to go under the supports for the Tappan Zee; I'd like to try for the main channel.

SD: Okay. Skip, you made six miles last night, no reason not to expect the same tonight. If current is up, we'll be golden; we'll make the bridge.

Sally: Bridge or bust!

SD (looking at his GPS, calling up to CP): Let's launch the dinghy; we're on location.

CP (putting his beer down): Righto.

SD (to CP): I'll get on the exact spot and you go ahead about 30 yards then dump Skip out.

Scene 2 Tappan Zee or bust
Scene opens with Tim and Sally on board the dinghy.
Tim (on VHF): Magic Moment, Magic Moment, this is the dinghy.
Ed (on VHF): Go ahead dinghy.
SD (on VHF): We're at the drop spot.
Ed (on VHF): We'll pull ahead.
SD (on VHF): You look good; have Skip enter the water.
(After Skip floats downstream to the dinghy)
Sally: Ready Skip, Go!
(After a bit)
SD: looks like we're headed for the right side of the channel.
SD (on VHF): Okay, I'm going to switch to 13 and make the *securité* announcement.
Ed (on VHF): I've all ready taken care of that.
SD (on VHF): Oh, thank you.
Ed (on VHF): Tug approaching would like you to stay on the green side of the channel.
SD (on VHF): I don't think we'll have any trouble with that.
SD: Sally, I'd like to head Skip for the bridge span just to the right of the main channel.
Sally: Should we bring him back?
SD: We're going to let him swim in this direction for a while; he's feeling the current.
Sally (blowing the whistle): Distance?
SD: Nine tenths. Was that the quarter-hour?
Sally: Yes.
SD: Not bad!
SS (speaking while stroking): Fumes!
SD: Sally, I'm switching sides.
Sally looks horrified at Tim.
SD: No, that's not what I meant. I'm just moving the boat to the other side of Skip.
SD moves the boat to the opposite side of the swimmer.
Sally: Tim, who is the most interesting swimmer to have swum the Hudson.
SD: That would be Steve Brodie. He was the first but he was actually following in the wake of another swimmer named Paul

Boyton who pioneered the swim. Paul swam it using a lifesaving suit that was a forerunner of today's survival suits.
Sally: What makes Steve interesting?
SD: He was the first person to jump off the Brooklyn Bridge and survive. It made him famous.
Sally: I never heard of him.
SD: That's because he made his jump three years after the Brooklyn Bridge was built, around 1886.
Sally: What's the big deal in that?
SD: The only other person to make the jump previously died. And I guess the two columns of his interview from his jail cell on the front page of the New York Times helped.
Sally: How'd he get into swimming?
SD: He was a lifeguard along the piers of Manhattan. After the jump, to exploit his fame, he exhibited himself in a nickel arcade at Coney Island.
Sally: Doesn't sound like you can make much doing that?
SD: Hey, this was before radio and television. Newspapers were kingmakers. He eventually made enough money to buy a bar on the Bowery. People doubted he did the jump so he displayed a certificate from the tugboat captain that pulled him out of the water on the wall at his bar.
Sally: So two years after jumping from the Brooklyn Bridge he swam the Hudson.
SD: Right, then the following year, and this isn't well known, he was the first person to go over Niagara Falls.
Sally: Isn't there a woman who's the first person over Niagara Falls around 1903? I forget her name.
SD: Sally, I know what you mean but I can only tell you what I read in the New York Times article about it. He was apprehended and convicted in Canadian court. They took testimony from witnesses!
Sally: This is unbelievable.
SD: The whole cottage industry surrounding Niagara Falls is going to have to retool. Think of all the wedding souvenirs purchased in Niagara Falls that have the wrong information on it.
Sally: Excuse me; I have to blow the whistle.
(Later, near the bridge)
SD: Have Skip swim away from the boat.
SS (stopping swimming): Tim, no good, I'm in an eddy!

SD: Skip, there's no eddies here!
(Skip puts his head down and swims on.)
SD: Sally, I don't know what he's talking about. Maybe he means an eddy off the bridge supports.
Sally: Maybe.
SD: I'd like to get him right thru the center of that bridge span.
(Skip passed as planned under the Tappan Zee)
SD: How much time do we have left?
Sally: About 20 minutes.
SD: Wow, looks like we'll be finishing up well south of the Tappan Zee. We'll keep him in if his speed is over 3 knots.
(Bit later)
SD: I haven't told you the most unbelievable story about Steve Brodie.
Sally: There's more?
SD: Yeah, he was an interesting guy.
Sally: All right, tell me the story.
SD: He said to have faked his own death.
Sally: What?
SD: Someone wrote a play about him and he was going around touring the country appearing in the play as his self.
Sally: All right.
SD: So when the play finished the run in Chicago, he was taking the train back to New York and the conductor couldn't wake him to take his ticket. I think he was had taken too many swigs of the bottle to wake up. So the conductor called ahead to New York to arrange for a coroner saying they were bringing the body back. Someone must have contacted the widow and she called the newspapers.
Sally: The New York Times, perhaps?
SD: Right, who ran an obituary the next day. Guess what day it was the story ran?
Sally: I don't know.
SD: April 1st, 1898, April Fools Day.
Sally: You're kidding me.
SD: No, they had to print a retraction on April 2nd. I just can't imagine the number of pints that got thrown back at his bar when Brodie showed up in New York alive and well on April 1st. What a party they must have had.
Sally: Tim, that's hilarious.

SD: I know, I was reading it over a hundred years later in the archives and I was howling with laughter when I suddenly realized the paper with the obituary ran on April Fools Day. Can you imagine the editor's concern when he finally died in 1901?
Sally: I wonder what the policy is on running a second obituary?
SD: I think the newspaper had a reporter put a stake thru the body to make sure he was dead.

(Later)
Sally (on VHF): Magic Moment, Magic Moment, just wanted to give you a little warning that I'm about to blow the signal horn.
CP (on VHF): Blow away.
CP and Ed are seen on the flying bridge of Magic Moment with their fingers in their ears, elbows akimbo to emphasis the gesture. SD laughs. Sally blows the signal horn twice.
Sally: Distance?
SD (gesturing): Six miles. Leave him in.
(12 minutes later)
SD: Okay, Sally, the speed has dropped. Signal him to get out.
Sally (blows signal horn three times): Yeah, Skip!
SD: Six and a half miles, Skip!
SS: Great swims, thank you everyone.
SD drops Sally off on Magic Moment.
CP: Take the dinghy in and put it on the dinghy dock.
SD: Oh, that'll be fun. I'll see what this baby can do.
SD (calling): Hey, Skip, thirty-six hours to the Tappan Zee Bridge. SS: We did it, Tim—you're the best.

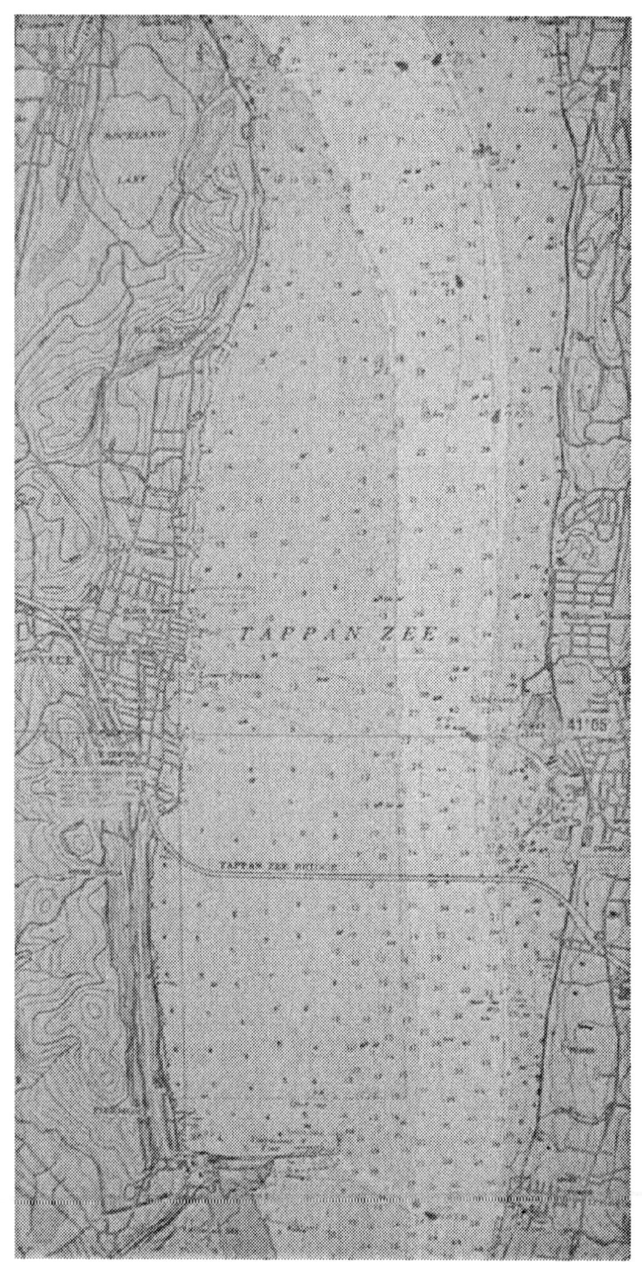

Stage 18 6.5 nautical miles.

Stage 19

Scene 1 Killing time

Wednesday, August 24th, PM swim with a 7 pm start. Weather: Blowing hard out of the north then it laid down and became calm after twilight. Starting location: 1.5 miles south of the Tappan Zee Bridge. Skip goes in around 7pm and rips off a 9.9-nautical mile swim in 2:37:39. Scene begins at Cornetta's Restaurant and Marina. Swim director is wearing the bright florescent yellow Skip Storch warm-up jacket from his 1988 swims. (SD is walking around the marina looking for people then wanders into the parking lot and sees Fred just pulling in)

SD: Fred, what 'cha up to?

Fred: I got a long lunch today and wanted to bring over the photos for everyone.

SD (looking at his watch): I think everyone is inside. Say, I need to find some sunglasses for the swim tonight. This morning when I ran the dinghy in, the water was so rough my sunglasses fell overboard

Fred: I can help you out after I see everyone; let me park my truck.

Fred (as Tim and Fred walk to the restaurant from the parking lot): There's RoJo (pointing) up on the lift. It looks like the engine problem was the transmission linkage.

(Inside Cornetta's is CP, Sally, and Ed. Tim and Fred grab some stools at the bar next to them)

Fred: Would you like anything to drink?

SD: Coke would be fine.

Fred (announcing to all): I've got photos for everyone.

Fred distributes CDs of his photos. Tim walks around the restaurant looking at the mounted fish on the walls and the photos. After a round of drinks and some idle chit-chat, Fred and Tim go off to find sunglasses.

About 3pm, Bryan Juncosa shows up. Tim, having returned from shopping was walking through the parking lot.

SD: Bryan, what 'cha doing?

Bryan: I'm just finishing gassing up my boat.

SD: Let me bring you inside and introduce you to everyone if they are still there. Are you going to be available tomorrow?

Bryan: Yes, I've cleared my calendar until the end of the swim.

SD: This is great.

SD (to CP): We're not going to need to use the dinghy again.
CP: Just fine. I checked the dinghy earlier and you actually did a good job storing the dinghy.
SD: Thanks; it seemed pretty obvious. I just had to be careful where I was stepping on that dock because of the ducks.
CP: Those filthy ducks, we can't get rid of them. Say, what time are we leaving?
SD: We're scheduled for a departure at 6:30pm. I believe that Channel 12 regional news is supposed to show up.
CP (jokingly): Let's keep an eye out for them.
SD: The average pace right now is two point eight five. We're closing in on the dog.
Sally: You mean the dog is still ahead of us?
SD: Technically, yes. For the past four swims we're been gaining on the dog one one-hundredth of a knot per swim.
(Around 4pm the crew gathers at Magic Moment, Kara has joined the group after finishing work.)
SD: Looks like Fred's boat is docked right over there.
Kara: Is he going out with us on the swim?
SD: No, but he'll be there for the finish. Where's Skip?
Sally: He went home for the afternoon.
SD: Not going to be doing much without the swimmer.
Sally: We're just hanging around waiting. What time is it?
SD: It's about 5pm. I'm going to take a look at the tides for tomorrow's swim down Manhattan.
(Tim pops inside to the salon and plops his computer up on the table, a bit later)
CP (pops his head in the cabin): It's six o'clock. Are we going to have a swim today?
SD: I hope so.
(Later, about 6:15pm)
SD: Here comes Skip now.
Skip comes down to the dock at the last moment with his wife.
SS: Tim, how are you? Good to see you. Is that my old jacket from the Long Island swim?
SD: Yes, it is.
SS: That was a long time ago.
SD: Yes it was. I thought I'd wear it to cheer you up.
SS (laughing): Geez, those were the day. Have you spoken to Jane lately?

SD: Yes, I consulted with her when I wrote the history of swimming book.
SS: Let's go over the swim. Do you have the charts?
SD: Here's where you left off. I've had Manny Sanguilly in these waters when he swam his Bridge to Bridge for the Asthma Foundation he organized for children and he just cruised down the Hudson. We were at the George Washington Bridge in four hours without even trying. The current in Manny's swim was still running. It may be possible for you to finish the swim tonight.
SS: We're at thirty-six hours right now.
SD: Correct.
SS: Well, I can't finish tonight because there would be no press at the finish. It'd be better to finish in the morning.
SD: We can do that.
SS: That's my best option for now.
SD: Then we'll split the swim in half and look to finish around Spuyten Duyvil.
SS: I need to get ready for the swim. Can you send Sally in?
SD: Let me gather up my stuff and the bench is all yours.
Skip and the girls retire to the salon.
SD: Andy, did you want to go out on the swim?
Andy: Tim, I grew up on the water but lately, I've become violently seasick whenever I'm on a boat.
SD: Then this is not the time to try some of the new medicine for motion sickness.
Andy (with a tinge of regret): No. I'll wave from shore.
Ed: Oh, look, here come the Regional News team.
CP (to camera crew): What happened the other day?
Spokesman: We got sent to a traffic accident.
Skip comes out from the salon and confers with the film crew.
SS: The video crew can't go out with us on the boat; they are going to film from Piermont Pier.
SD: You've five minutes until departure.
Camera crew quickly sets up and starts interviewing Skip.
I'm going over to Bryan's boat. Sally, is it you or Kara that coming with me?
Sally: Me!
SD: The boat is down the pier toward…
Sally: Tim, I was on the boat last night!

SD: Oh, yeah. I think the days are beginning to blur together on me.
Sally: Well you better not get too blurry eyed with all the duck poop around or you will slip and fall into the water.
(At Bryan's boat a few piers down from Magic Moment)
SD: Where's Bryan?
Sally: I don't know.
SD: Here he comes.
Bryan: We'll cast off as soon as I start the engines.

Scene 2 Monster swim
The crew rides out in two boats, Magic Moment with Kara aboard and Bryan's boat where Tim and Sally are.
SD: We did great this morning to get this far south of the Tappan Zee.
Bryan: Considering where I left you off last night, I'm surprised.
SD: We stopped this morning right by the buoys. Let me check the GPS…we need to go 200 yards north.
Bryan: Okay.
SD (on VHF): Magic Moment, we're pulling ahead about 200 yards, I would like you to move upstream of us when we stop and drop Skip in the water.
Ed: We'll pull ahead when you stop.
SD (to Bryan): Okay, we're in the vicinity, here is as good as any. Try and hold the boat in position against the current.
Bryan: Right.
SD (moving up to the bow with Sally): I've noticed that the time he needs to get acclimated to the water has decreased so let's give him a start as soon as possible.
Sally (calling): Skip, three, two, one, Go.
Sally blows signal horn.
SD: The wind is light airs out of the north; we're going to have trouble with fumes.
Bryan: Could you drop the drag into the water?
SD (fusses with the lines, begins feeding the towline out when it goes overboard): I've lost the towline!
Bryan (looking back): We can pick it up. I'll circle around.
SD: I think I released one end of the bridle when I let out on the towline.

Bryan (pulling the Staples carton from the water): Well, here it is. Let's catch up with Skip.
SD refastens the lines and drops the drag in the water.
Sally (blows whistle): Tim, what's the distance?
SD: Three tenths a mile in five minutes, nothing spectacular.
Sally: I use to live up there.
SD: Where is that?
Sally: Dobbs Ferry in those apartments overlooking the water.
Sally (to Bryan): Do you have binoculars?
Bryan: Let me search around for them. Here they are.
Sally: I'm going to take a look.
SD: What would you be looking at?
Sally: My ex-girlfriend. I left her.
SD: Are you spying on her? Do you think she has someone else?
Sally: Not a chance.
SD: Sally, it looks to me like you are jealous.
Sally doesn't answer. She continues to scan the building along shore for about two minutes.
Sally: It's hard to put things in the past when you invest so much time in them.
SS: Fumes!
SD (Looking at the engines momentarily to observe the smoke): Bryan, there is a slight amount of drifting smoke. Let switch sides.
Bryan: Okay. I'll let him swim ahead of us then pull up on his other side.
SD: Fine. With this wind, when we're crossing it'll just blow down on him. Nothing we can do about that.
Bryan: How about if I keep him just slightly to our stern.
SD: We can try it.
(Bit later)
SD: I think I'll call Magic Moment and caution them to stay ahead of us in case he's picking up their exhaust.
(Later, as night falls, the lights are rigged over the side)
SD: It's hard to pick out the course. Do you see the next buoy?
Bryan: I'm headed up on the cluster of lights off the starboard bow.
Sally (blowing the signal horn): Distance?
SD: Three point seven miles in one hour.

Sally: Fabulous.
SD: That is great!
Sally: Are we leaving him in or pulling him at two hours?
SD: I'm hoping that he can make Spuyten Duyvil before the current drops.
Bryan: It's not too far off.
Sally (excited): I can see the George Washington Bridge now.
Bryan (to SD): I've been on every major bridge in metropolitan NY from top to bottom inspecting them.
SD: You mean the footings?
Bryan: I inspect the underwater portion and report on their conditions. Here's my card.
SD: So you're a diver (reading the card) and a professional engineer. I'm the president of the Massachusetts Society of Professional Engineers.
Bryan: No kidding.
(Later)
Sally (blowing the signal horn): Its two hours. Distance?
SD: Seven point seven miles. He's done 4 miles in one hour.
Bryan: When should we pull him?
SD: When we see the Spuyten Duyvil railroad bridge. His speed is way over 3 knots. He's killing!
(Later)
SD (to Bryan): I think it possible for a swimmer to start at the Tappan Zee Bridge and swim all the way to the Battery on one tide. Then, the swimmer does a regular Manhattan marathon swim all the way around Manhattan. At that point, they've gone about 50 miles without stopping and it's all current-aided.
Bryan: Has anybody done it?
SD: Not yet.
Sally: Coming up on two and a half hours.
Sally blows the signal horn.
SD: Nine point four miles. We're slowing down.
Bryan: Here's Spuyten Duyvil.
SD: Sally, wait for the railroad bridge to come up even with us then let's get him out.
SD (on VHF): Magic Moment, Magic Moment, we're about to pull him out. You could take up position momentarily.
Ed (on VHF): Will do.
SD (on VHF): Swim start tomorrow is seven AM.

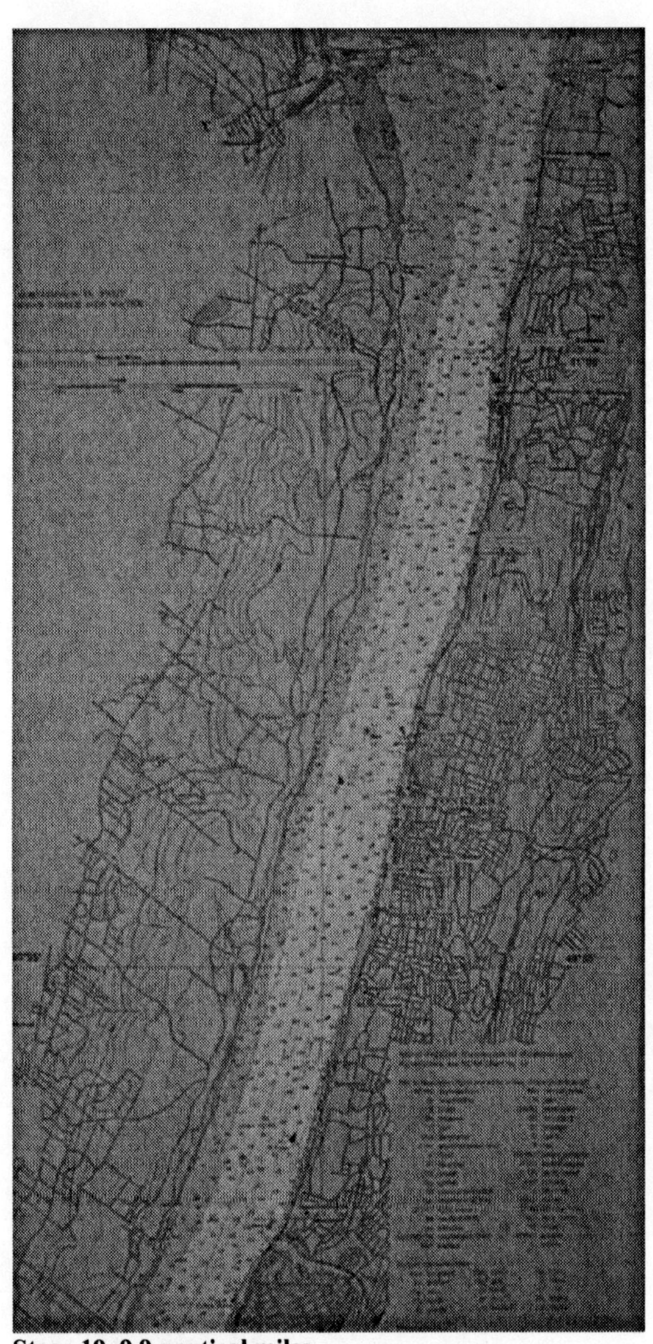

Stage 19 9.9 nautical miles.

Stage 20

Scene 1 A swim to die for

Thursday, August 25th, AM swim with a 7 am scheduled start. Weather was 10-knot wind out of the north with some gusts; modest wave action in the water and clear skies overhead. Location of the start is off Spuyten Duyvil at the northernmost location of Manhattan at 7:12am. Support team is Magic Moment, No Name, and Red Grenier's Sunset. To be joined later by Roger in his Grady White. Scene opens aboard Bryan's boat with SD, Sally and Kara aboard.

Skip (from the stern of Magic Moment): Now?

SD: Yes, this is where we left off.

Skip launches himself into the river just off Spuyten Duyvil.

Sally: Ready, Go. (Blows signal horn).

SD (to Sally): Good start.

Bryan: Tim, can you throw the drogue in?

Tim: Okay.

Tim tosses the plastic Staples file carton over the side and feeds out the dragline.

Kara: How long until the finish?

SD: The best I'd expect him to do is 4 hours but I told him a 3 ½ is possible just to get him to agree to do the swim in one shot.

Bryan: Skip wanted us ahead of him if our engine fumes were going to drift down on him.

SD: With this wind out of the north, that means he has to look up to see us. That stresses his neck. Let me see if I can slip this red fender ball over the dragline so he can look at that when he swims.

Tim fusses with the lines and the buoy slip 50 feet behind the boat.

(later)

SD (on VHF): Magic Moment, Magic Moment, this is the Big Dink. (Pause) Magic Moment, Magic Moment, this is the Big Dink.

SD hands the VHF to the girls

SD (to Kara): See if you can find out the water temperature.

Kara (to VHF): Magic Moment, Magic Moment this is Little Dink and Bow Babe.

CP: Go ahead, my little dink.

Kara: Could you let me know the water temperature?

CP: We have it right here, its 77 degrees.
Kara: Thank you.
SD: Why don't I just leave that radio with you girls?
Sally: Sounds good.
Sally and Kara launch into a noisy chatter with each other. Sally is perched on the bow.
(Later, under the George Washington Bridge)
SD: Sally, could you write down the time we're going under the GW Bridge.
Sally: Got it.
SD (reading the GPS): We're hitting 4 knots!
Bryan: Anything unusual about that.
SD: Yes, it's tremendous for a swimmer. I was thinking of taking him wide over to the Jersey side because the Hudson bends to the left but at this speed there is no need.
Kara (blows signal horn): what's the distance?
SD: One point seven miles.
SD (to Bryan): The speed isn't agreeing with the distance.
(Later)
Kara (blows signal horn): what's the distance?
SD: Three point seven miles. Is that the first hour?
Kara: Yes.
SD (in exclamation): This confirms the 4-knot reading we got earlier. If we go 2 miles in a half hour, we're holding the 4 knots. We'll be at the finish before eleven am.
Girls: Wow, spectacular (…further babble).
(Later)
Cell phone rings
Sally: Tim, if that Skip's wife, don't answer it.
SD: Sally, that's kind of hard to do…
SD (on cell phone): Andy, how are you?
Andy (on cell phone): Tim, you have to stop the swim. Skip is sick.
SD (on cell phone): What?
Andy (on cell phone); He's not going to be able to finish.
SD (on cell phone): Andy, he looking great right now. Why do you say this?
Andy (on cell phone): We had chicken last night and I just threw up.

SD (on cell phone, slowly): Okay, he's swimming fine right now; I'll keep an eye on him.
Andy (on cell phone): Thank you, Tim.
SD (on cell phone): The chicken might have affected you differently than Skip.
Andy (on cell phone): I'm counting on you.
SD (on cell phone): No problem, take care, good-bye.
SD (to Bryan): I didn't want to tell Andy but I've seen swimmers throw up right in the water.
Bryan: Oh, that's disgusting.
SD: Skip is going to finish this. He smells victory.
Girls: Go, Skip, Go!
SD: It looks like we'll hold 4 knots until the last half hour when we are down by the World Trade Center when it'll slow down.
(Later)
SD (to Bryan): The boys on Magic Moment are getting some cooperation from NY Waterways. Their ferries are slowing down when they come by us. That's unusual.
SS (stopped swimming): What's that blocking my path?
SD: Carnival Line cruise ship. It's docking. Keep swimming.
SS: What?
Girls: Cruise ship; keep going.
SS resumes stroking
(Later)
Bryan (to VHF): We're on the water, just passing the Intrepid right now.
SD: Who is that?
Bryan: Roger coming out in his boat. I've known Roger since high school. Roger introduced me to Skip.
SD: I remember Skip talking about Roger. I've just never met him.
(Later)
SD: The World Trade Center wall is coming into view. We'll need to start moving him over to the wall.
Sally: What wall?
SD: It's the wall up ahead (pointing)
Sally: Tim, don't point.
SD: See if you can move him closer to the boat.
Sally hands Kara her phone and gestures. Skip looks up and keeps swimming straight.

SD: Bryan, we're going to have to move to his right side to move him over closer to Manhattan.
Bryan: Keep an eye on the drogue.
SD: Right.
(Little bit later)
Sally: Does he know what the wall is?
SD: They all do, he's swum Manhattan before. In the last stages, swimmers hug the bulkhead wall of the WTC and blast down to the finish on a current. Just with the new World Trade Center ferry terminal slip we have to hold them out until we're past that point.
SD (to Bryan): Hold him out here until we're past that work barge and buoy south of the ferry slip.
(Once past)
SD: Signaling him to swim away from the boat.
SD (shouting to Skip): The wall, swim to the wall.
Girls: The wall, the wall.
SS swim over by the wall and Bryan positions his boat to starboard of Skip.
SD (to Bryan): Up ahead, where the wall turns left toward the East River, swing around in front of him so he doesn't swim off away from the wall.
SD: The fireboat house has a dead spot, an eddy, between the end of the wall and the pier itself. That's where John van Wisse re-captured the lead over Bronwen Whitehead in the 2001 Manhattan Island Swim Marathon.
Bryan: How'd he do that?
SD: He stayed on the outside of Whitehead by a few yards and when she swam into the dead water, he took just two strokes and passed her. They were both Australians and John just loved rough water. He made up over a mile in less than an hour when the Hudson turned choppy that day. He was that far behind.
(Passing the restored Battery Fireboat house)
Bryan: Where do we bring him in?
SD (looking at the new ferry terminal slip at slip B): Right past the Lost Mariners Monument is some open space.
Sally: Where should he go?
SD: Dead ahead, have him touch the wall.
Sally (gesturing): Touch the wall.
SD: What's the official time?

Sally (marking the time): 2 hours, 55 minutes, 29 seconds.
SD: He broke three hours for the Manhattan Hudson River shoreline. Remarkable!
SD: Sally, call Magic Moment to pick Skip up.
SS (swimming back out to Magic Moment): Any photographers?
SD: I see one. (To Bryan) Let's pull up closer and see if he needs any information.
SD (to photog): That's Skip Storch, his time down the Hudson broke 42 hours.
Photog: Can you have him swim in from the Statute?
SD: No problem.
SS also posed Charles Atlas style on the back of Magic Moment for the press. This photo appeared in the paper the next day with the title: Stud of the Hudson. (Later)
SD (to Bryan): See any more press?
Bryan: There are some people over there.
SD: They look like amateurs, the professional photographers always wear vest.
SD (to VHF): Looks like that's it for the press.
CP (on VHF): Time to head back up to Cornetta's.
SD (on VHF): I know Roger is anxious to have Skip stop in Hoboken for a photo op with the Mayor.
Roger (on VHF): I'm sure I can get the mayor there and the local press.
CP (on VHF): Skip okay with it. Let's do it.
Bryan and Roger take off racing their boat back upriver snapping pictures of each other as their boat go over each other's wakes.

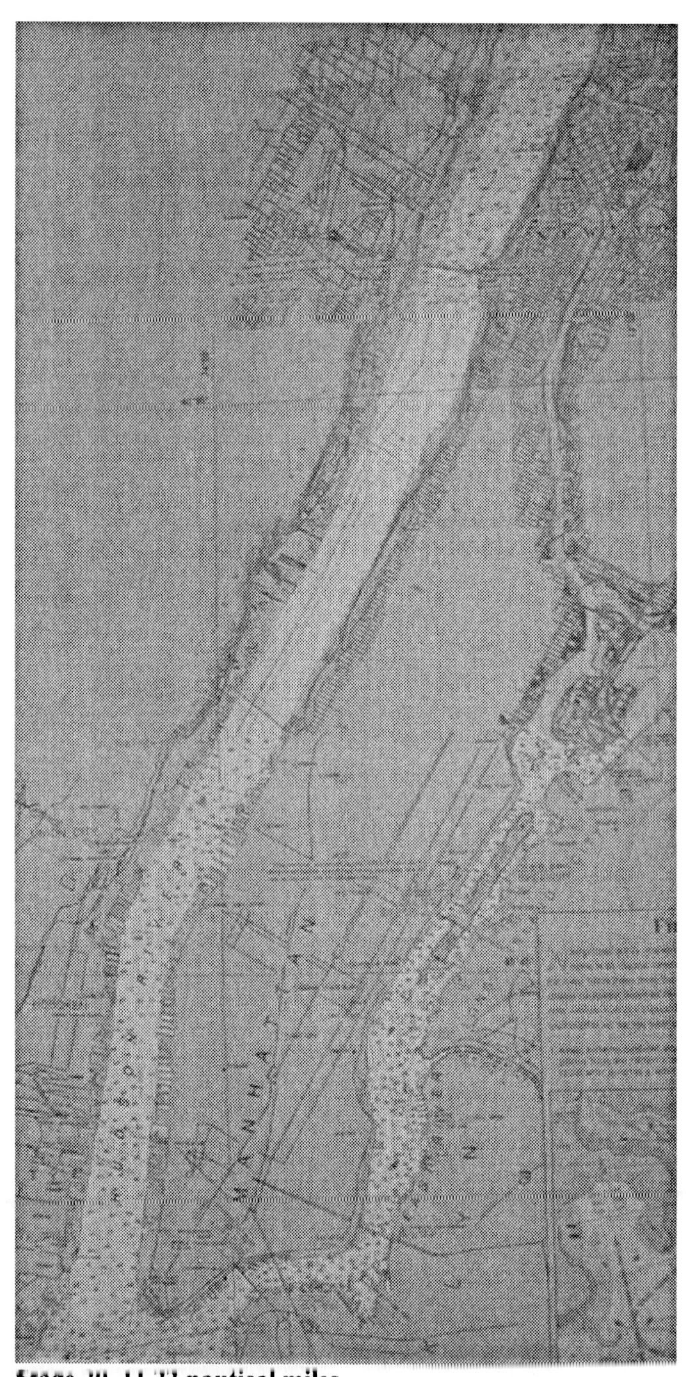

Stage 20 11.22 nautical miles.

Epilogue

Scene: in a side corner of a living room the SD is before a portable computer at a secretariat. It's late at night during the fall of 2005. The SD is reading charts of the Hudson. He's alone on the stage; half the stage is darken. The phone rings.
SD: Skip, I was just about to call you.
SS: Tim, I wanted to thank you again for helping out.
SD: Skip, I loved every minute of it.
SS: What made this swim special was the way we worked together.
SD: You handled a lot. More than once I remember you telling us to go get something to eat and not worrying about yourself.
SS: I knew how to handle issues and most of them were related to money. People's comfort is important and team members had to pace themselves. Did you see what the New York Post called me: Stud of the Hudson.
SD (chuckling): Yes, I did. I couldn't believe it. This puts you up there with the Kentucky Derby winners being put out to pasture.
SS: Hey, that's not fair, the horses make more money.
SD (forcefully): Skip, the river taught us how to swim it.
SS: What do you mean?
SD: The first stage was a disaster. We got back on track because the river reset itself to normal. Then I learned that I had to check the current nearly every time we went out. A lot of times it was okay but there were a few times that we had to delay your starts.
SS: Right, I remember.
SD: The adjustments we made reminded me of a slinky toy. It's was as if the current took a hit at the start then that effect went up and down the river causing changes to the tide all along the length.
SS: Interesting.
SD: I think we got only 50% of the rated current in the upper reaches no matter what we did. My initial estimate I sent you didn't even come close to being correct. That's why I was figuring out the swim stage by stage for the first week. After Bear Mountain Bridge, maybe it was a higher salinity count or something but you started doing six miles on a regular basis.
SS: Where do you think the current went?

SD: I don't know. We tried everything and it wasn't that wide up there. If there was anyplace we'd lose the current, I thought it would be going through Haverstraw Bay but those swims were great!
SS: That's my home turf!
SD: The last two swim were spectacular. That's where you passed the dog.
SS: You mean the average speed.
SD: Yup, the dog averaged two point nine knots.
SS: That was one fast dog! What was my average?
SD: Three point one knots.
SS: Wow!
SD: I knew you'd do it because the dog took 22 days.
SS: How's that?
SD: The fast tides only last 2 weeks. That meant the dog had a week of slow tides.
SS: So we had a built-in guarantee I'd set the record?
SD: Yes, but after that start, I was worried. Then the upper Hudson didn't deliver and I started to doubt we'd do it. But you killed from the Tappan Zee down.
SS: Manhattan is so familiar to me having swum it so many times.
SD: The River is going to do what it's going to do. We're incidental to the flow, we just happen to be paddling about in it.
SS: True, but I was glad you were there looking out for me.
SD: Best ten days of my life; but was I tired afterwards! It took me three days to catch up on my sleep.
SS: Same here.
SD: I sent an email to Tammy van Weiss telling her I don't know how she did the Murray River swim.
SS: She's the Australian that swam 1500 miles in 106 days?
SD: Right. In a swim that long they count the days, hours are meaningless.
SS: That's impressive.
SD: What's next?
SS: I was thinking about a triple around Manhattan…

About the Author

Timothy M. Johnson grew up in California and graduated from Fontana High School in 1964. He swam and played water polo for Coach Al Zamsky after learning to swim at age 14. He attended the US Merchant Marine Academy at Kings Point, New York, and swam on their Division III swim team. Leaving the academy to start a family he joined New York Telephone Company and served in their Special Services division as an FCC Licensed Radio Technician for microwave and video communications links. During the 1970's he participated in the Marriage Encounter apostolate with his wife as a team couple. He participated in the formation of the Manhattan Island Swimming Association and played supporting roles through the 1980's and 90's and has been tangentially involved ever since leading to his designation as historian for the organization in 2004. His knowledge of swimming combined with navigation learned at the Academy led to a number of relationships with swimmers and together they explored the frontiers of swimming. His interest in academics and studies lead to the development of specialized computer applications that modeled swims allowing analysis of marathon swims that was unprecedented. Prior to moving to Cape Cod in 1996, he completed a Masters in Electrical Engineering program at New York Institute of Technology and passed the exam for a Coast Guard Masters license 100 tons, steam or sail, towing endorsement. Since this time he has registered as a professional engineer, teaches at Wentworth Institute of Technology, and served as president of the Massachusetts Society of Professional Engineer 2004-2005. During the summers he teaches coastal navigation for Boston Harbor Sailing Club. He is an active Rotarian and has formed a company, Captain's Engineering Services Inc., for the publication of inexpensive textbooks.

Printed in the United States
47200LVS00005B/301-336

9 780972 172639